Clearing Land

CLEARING LAND

Legacies of the American Farm

JANE BROX

NORTH POINT PRESS

A division of Farrar, Straus and Giroux

New York

North Point Press
A division of Farrar, Straus and Giroux
19 Union Square West, New York 10003

Some of the names in this book have been changed.

Grateful acknowledgment is made to the following for permission to reprint previously published material:
"On a Raised Beach—The Bonxie with the Herring Fishers" by Hugh Mac-Diarmid, from *Selected Poetry*, copyright © 1992 by Michael Grieve. Reprinted by permission of New Directions Publishing Corp.
Excerpt from *The Shape of Time* by George Kubler, copyright © 1962 by Yale University. Used by permission of Yale University Press.
"Horses," from *Collected Poems* by Edwin Muir, copyright © 1960 by Willa Muir. Used by permission of Oxford University Press; also from *Selected Poems of Edwin Muir* by Edwin Muir. Used by permission of Faber and Faber Ltd.
Excerpt from "Mending Wall" from *The Poetry of Robert Frost*, edited by Edward Connery Lathem. Copyright 1915, 1930, 1939, 1969 by Henry Holt and Company, © 1967 by Lesley Frost Ballantine, © 1958 by Robert Frost. Reprinted by permission of Henry Holt and Company, LLC.

Library of Congress Cataloging-in-Publication Data
Brox, Jane, 1956–
    Clearing land : legacies of the American farm / Jane Brox.— 1st ed.
        p.   cm.
    Includes bibliographical references.
    ISBN-13: 978-0-86547-649-3
    ISBN-10: 0-86547-649-7 (hardcover : alk. paper)
    1. Brox, Jane, 1956– Family. 2. Brox family. 3. Family farms—Merrimack River Valley (N.H. and Mass.) 4. Farm life—Merrimack River Valley (N.H. and Mass.) 5. Merrimack River Valley (N.H. and Mass.)—Biography. I. Title.

    CT274.B779B756 2007
    974.4'5—dc22

                                                        2003028114

Designed by Jonathan D. Lippincott

www.fsgbooks.com

1   3   5   7   9   10   8   6   4   2

For my mother, Antoinette Brox

Our signals from the past are very weak, and our means for recovering their meaning still are most imperfect . . . The beginnings are much hazier than the endings, where at least the catastrophic action of external events can be determined . . . Now and in the past, most of the time the majority of people live by borrowed ideas and upon traditional accumulations, yet at every moment the fabric is being undone and a new one is woven to replace the old, while from time to time the whole pattern shakes and quivers, settling into new shapes and figures. These processes of change are all mysterious uncharted regions where the traveler soon loses direction and stumbles in darkness.

—George Kubler, *The Shape of Time*

Contents

Clearing Land

INHERITANCE

Horseman, pass by, I used to whisper as the sirens made their long way down the road from the center of town. Now: one, two, three, four, five, six, seven gone out of a generation—my father, both his sisters, four of his six brothers. They had possessed a collective strength that gave definition not only to the family but to the farm itself, to the hundred acres of woods and streambeds, fields and orchards we have called ours that lie across the worn coastal hills north of Boston. I know time itself helped to establish a sense of security, time in place, time and a generation's fidelity to each other. Even as six of the brothers married and moved on and the care of the farm passed to my own father, there was a particular bond among all those siblings that lasted their entire lives. In their later, quieter years, though the farmhouse was no longer the gathering place for the extended family at holidays, all of my uncles were still in and out of it, often almost daily. In the years before his death my father lingered long at the table by the kitchen window, exchanging the news of the family, of the day. I can see him there still, bent over the local paper, talking with his sister Bertha.

That no one in the family lives in the old farmhouse anymore may be the strangest thing about all these passings. For almost a hundred years its nineteenth-century forthrightness had been at our center, and had so worked into our imaginations that, more frequently than I look at any of the pictures of my ancestors, I contemplate the 1901 photograph of the farmhouse with its linkage of buildings: summer kitchen, carriage house, barn. As I study the blades of the windmill above the roofline and imagine the silo just out of the frame, the world appears sturdy against a backdrop of sober daylight. A patient horse is swaddled in ropes and harnesses. Men and women look up from their work in the muddy yard. *However it is in some other world*, their uncomplaining gazes seem to say, *I know that this is the way in ours.* Farming in New England was already in decline, with woods growing up on long-cleared lands as the mill cities and prospects to the west pulled people away from this countryside, but it was still the common life, wide open under a big sky, and one farm's holdings adjoined those of the next and the next all down the road—pasture and field and orchard extending as far as the eye could see.

Scrawled across the back of my copy of the photograph in my father's hand is *Brox Farm 1901*, so for a long time I'd imagined it to depict a moment just after my grandparents took possession of the place, after their emigration from Lebanon, after peddling wares in upstate New York, and briefly enduring tenement life in the city of Lawrence six miles to the east of the farm. Even when I learned that it actually captures the last days of ownership of the family who'd lived there before my grandparents, it hardly seemed to matter. My family had simply taken over a way of life that had been accumulating for centuries, and there was little enough difference between last days and first.

In the years after my grandparents came into possession of the farm, the windmill blew down, the silo burned, but one after another child was born, the size of the milk herd increased, and their halting English became more certain. In time, teams of ordinary horses gave way to tractors as the farm steadied into the one I knew where irises and roses flourished at the fence, full-grown shade trees tossed high above the roof peak in the storms, and my entire extended family—thirty, forty of us—would gather at the farmhouse during the holidays. Aunts, uncles, cousins crowded the kitchen and dining room. We ate Lebanese *kibbeh* and stuffed grape leaves, we tore off pieces of Syrian bread to scoop up *hummous bi tahini*. The heat chuffed, the warm air was filled with voices, while beyond us, beyond the watery old glass of the farmhouse windows, the world was bright with the stark New England winter.

That the farmhouse remained for so long at the center of our world surely had to do with the fact that my aunts, Bertha and Del, who never married, lived there all their lives, along with my bachelor Uncle Joe. My brothers and male cousins have little anecdotes even now about Joe. He taught them how to check a tire for leaks and how to change the oil in a truck. He stood over them as they planted the tulip bulbs in the farmhouse yard under his direction: "Is that hole four inches deep?" "Four inches," any boy would affirm. "Bulb on its side?" "Bulb on its side." But it's Bertha and Del whom I recall most often. When I was very young the farmhouse had been—like the meadow, the brook, the woods—one of the stations of my childhood. I would go there almost daily with one or three or four of my girl cousins who lived near me. We tracked in mud, we tracked in snow. We spoke of them— Auntie Bertha and Auntie Del—in the same breath, as if one word. It seemed all the noise there ever was we brought with us into the kitchen as we settled in the rockers and easy chairs or around the table by the east windows where we found our- selves bent over Scrabble with Bertha or searching through the puzzle pieces laid out and partially interlocked. The unen- tered rooms, made more still by our games in the kitchen, were sometimes peopled by the recollection of evenings when there were so many for supper they had to eat in shifts at the oak table—a silver cup full of silver spoons at its center—or of the living room thick with cigar smoke when the brothers had brought friends home after a late night out.

The apples blossomed, the grass dried in the August heat, my aunts' attention continued to turn to the sound of a car pulling into the drive, to the tenor of their brothers' voices hailing them as they walked up the porch stairs. In time my own world became crowded with life beyond the farm, with friends from high school and dreams of going away—it's hard to remember when I hadn't been intent on going away. I bent to my books during those late teenage nights, my imagining and hopes running on faster than the frequencies on the radio dial I flipped through when I was restless: static, voices, snatches of song, everything in the world there if you could just tune in, if you could just settle on the right place . . . My visits to my aunts became less spontaneous then, more brief and formal, made dutifully, prodded by my parents. I sat stiffly by the window, feeling the stillness of the house now that the games had fallen away. The family pride—"You don't act that way . . ." "Remember who you are . . ."—began to feel far too confining, and I tried not to stir it up as Del sat there rocking and Bertha knitted panels in patterns of cable and box stitches to make afghans for each departing niece to take away to college. I wondered about their single lives, their devotion to the family, the protection and regard of their brothers, the way you wonder about those flocks of swifts you see in late August, readying themselves, making their glinting turns in the turbulent air—are they helped by the wind or made helpless by it?

"I'd sell pies and ice cream," Bertha recalled, her needles clicking into the quiet as she told me about the tearoom her father had built for her to run just across the road from the farmhouse. She elaborated on the story during later visits: "We called it the Red Wing—everyone along the road would stop in . . ." I can still hear her mild, soft chuckle, and a final comment: "Anything to keep me home." Then she turned again to the work in her lap, which by then may even have been my own afghan in shades of blue that I was to drape over myself as I read poetry and studied ecosystems, Shake-speare, and Russian history in my cinder-block dorm room al-most two hundred miles away.

Del was the first of that generation to die. When the cancer was diagnosed she was set and determined to begin with. "I want to know the news, however bad," they say she told the doctors. Then came the affront of treatment: "They made me drink barium." She'd always carried her large self with dig-nity, had carried out everything with deliberate care, even something as small as shaping Easter cookies, hundreds each the same size and intricately shaped. Her generation of the family did not record much, but everything worth noting is set down in her meticulous, flourished hand, every wedding notice and obituary of the extended family—third cousins, cousins twice removed—clipped and pasted by her into a hardbound album. I don't remember her ever registering fear, even as her voice grew faint and hoarse. "I've had a good life," she said to me squarely. In the later stages of her illness she began to shrink rapidly in her dresses. A stairlift appeared on the farmhouse stairs. She became a frail shape, unimaginable even to herself: "Who'd ever have thought I could feel my bones against the seat of the chair?" she said in a kind of wonder.

"You should come back for a visit now," my father told me one day, and then he went on to warn me I might not recognize her. I had been living away for years by then while my father and brother carried on the work of the farm. At the time I was on Nantucket Island, thirty miles off the coast of Massachusetts, so the return felt like a real journey. The ferry pulled away from the dock in the harbor dawn and glided past the last sandy stretches of wild, scoured land, then past cormorants drying themselves on the jetties. It took hours to cross the sound then, and after the quiet suspended world of us travelers—just our murmurs and the humming engines—I was always startled by the bright, jostling morning of the working world when I debarked on the Cape. However quiet the ferry had been, it couldn't compare to how tamped down the farm felt when I arrived back that time. My aunt's failing was all the concern. Small helpless gestures: her brothers would bring her boiled lobster—one of the few things she could keep down—and they'd urge her to eat just a little something. She might pick at the meat in the legs or at the fine white flakes in the cavity of the body before pushing it aside. The few deaths I'd endured until then had been sudden. I'd never seen anyone passing out of the world before.

When I returned a few weeks later for the funeral and stepped out of the car on a warm, clear summer morning—the sky: a white haze on blue—I was startled that the farmhouse appeared as serene as always. With the rows of tasseling corn and trellised tomatoes following the curve of the old hills, the placid geometry of the farm had never seemed so absolute before. Whether heightened by contrast to my life away or by death, or both, I can't say. I only know how set and ordered the farm appeared so early in June—always the most perfect time, when all is hoped for and full of energy, before drought sets in, and small failures—and I seemed to see for the first time the kind of care it took to keep up the place. I swear I remember it that way, though the last time I was at the family grave site I saw that Del had died in winter, and my sister insists she was then nearly nine months pregnant with my nephew, who was born in January.

I've lost track of the time between that first death and my return to the farm to help out—was it fours years, or six, seven?—but I'm sure Del's passing and the way I remember the farm having appeared to me that day played a part in my decision. Perhaps it's only that the sense it aroused of a place steady, assured, and vulnerable had begun to meet my wish for some definition in my life. Already time had worn on my desire for freedom, or had made that desire seem ordinary. Nantucket had given way to other places, to western Massachusetts, to towns outside Boston where the wail of sirens was

anonymous to me. I'd seen many of my friends marry and begin to establish families of their own. With Del's death, maybe
I began to recognize the fragility of my one and only family,
and the farm. My father and brother had always had their dif-
ferences concerning the running of things, my brother wanting to expand for the future with a larger farmstand and
greenhouses, wanting to experiment with methods and crops;
my father, more cautious. As my brother fell further into the
drugs he'd begun using as a teenager, his ideas were paired
with an unreliability that worsened the contentions between
them. In my years away I'd tried to ignore the arguments—I
felt helpless in the face of them—but with the family growing
old, they began to seem consequential.

Whatever else my return to the farm has meant for my
life, it has made the later years of that older generation
more clear to me than their earlier ones, none more so than
Bertha's. I can't imagine her life beyond the farm. I know she
traveled when she was younger and spent some summers
working in a resort—in the Adirondacks, was it? But the life I
knew was defined by her singular fidelity, and the fidelity it
engendered in return.

After my father and four of my uncles had followed Del to
their graves, Bertha sometimes forgot that they had gone, and
I had to tell her again that Stanley had passed away, and again
her eyes registered the grief as clearly as the first time it had
been told to her. She was in her nineties by then, and a neighbor had moved in to help her with daily life. She had bristled
at the thought of someone outside the family coming into the

farmhouse, but she no longer had the strength to refuse. Joe's plaid coat and creased hat still hung on the coatrack. The dresses of Del's large, healthy self still hung in the closet. Bertha wouldn't have it any other way. "I like to have my familiar things around me," she said, standing stooped among the stove and sink and counters where she'd spent so much of her life working steadily at four things at once if need be: leveling off the measured flour with the blade of a knife, punching down dough in an earthenware bowl, saving the chicken fat, saving scraps. Always at the end of my brief visits, after I'd filled the air with patter about small things—the growing season, the weather—and had repeated myself just to keep the air stirring, after I'd said I should be going, she'd query me: "What's your hurry?" I could feel the silence I would leave behind me.

Her last summer was full of heat and drought. Amid the late terse calls of gathering birds, pine branches cracked overhead as squirrels collected nuts for their stores. The irrigation ponds had been pumped down to nothing and still there wasn't enough water for the corn. The apples reddened small, the honey darkened to a flavor deeper than I'd ever tasted, and by September the air smelled of ripe grapes on one wind, and on another of the dust that swirled in back of the pickups. We began to discern a new map of our world, one on which all the susceptible, stressed places in the land stood out: the younger maples and the ones by the road where the soil was laden with salt began to brown before they had a chance to flame with their fall colors. Each leaf dried up, from the edges in. The last green of the year lingered in the low marshy places. Bertha was always by the window when I stopped by, and every few minutes she'd gaze up at the unmitigated hard blue above and say, "Look, what a beautiful day, not a cloud in the sky."

Toward the end of that growing season she rarely had the strength to keep her place at the window and began to spend most of her time lying on a bed that had been brought downstairs and set up in the old summer kitchen. The shades were drawn against the sun; she: half sleeping, small. Still, no one else could touch the strength she got from her remaining brothers as they stood saddened and bewildered in front of her. She seemed less than half aware of me by then, as I chattered on about the world as it was, how the winter rye was coming up everywhere now. What was I talking for? To keep her in this world? To keep myself from wondering about her life, steeped in its certain fidelity, which led me to think of my own now lived for its own fidelities? Once I grew ashamed of my patter, and said simply, "Well, this is pretty tough." She focused her clouded eyes on me, shook her head with surprising strength, and uttered a deep, imperious "ohhhhh," and I blanched and looked away, knowing I didn't know the half of it.

Her two surviving brothers spent a long painful time trying to sum up her life for the local paper, to conjure up something beyond the household. "Have them list all the nieces and nephews," one of my uncles said to me. "Remember she was a seamstress for a while, have them put that in." Her funeral was quiet, and maybe twenty-five of us—my cousins and siblings and their scattering of children and teenagers, a few old friends of the family, the priest—went back to the farmhouse afterward for a meal in the backyard. It was a beautiful June day to begin with, though a thunderstorm came in from the west and we all rushed into the close, bright kitchen. The house smelled of our dank hair and clothes and the rain brought out a little must. Someone opened a window for air, the curtains billowed in the wind, and we could hear the downpour and thunder as we dried ourselves off and poured ourselves coffee. We talked on and on about the house, the times, our own childhoods, the whole long lives of them all. "She would have liked this," one of us said. That turned out to be the last time we gathered as a family in the farmhouse. It took a good while for anyone to think of what to do with all the things, and the clothes of the three of them hung in the closets for the longest time. Afterward, when I would see a cousin of mine, one of us would say: "It's so strange not to have them there." And the other: "I know."

The farm, if you were to drive by it now, would appear as measured and ordered as ever, even though no one in the family works the land anymore. I'd stopped helping out the year before my father died: the antagonism between my brother and him had just been too difficult for me. My brother didn't carry on for more than a year after my father's death. I think for all his grief—his was probably the most complex grief of all—he'd imagined a freedom for himself after my father died, though he was to find he was no more heir to the farm than anyone else. He had siblings to contend with, and uncles. His chances would never be clear, what with all the family history behind the farm. His own difficult past had made us all wary of trusting him with the running of the place, even though no one else knew enough or had the time or desire to see to it: a small farm had become an intricate

business, and with the costs of owning land, the taxes and in-
surance, just letting it be wasn't an option. In today's world a
farm isn't often abandoned to woods. Some other human
scheme is waiting.

In hopes of keeping the farm going I eventually made a call
to one of the countless boys who'd worked for my father over
the years to ask if he would come back. David had worked on
the farm all through high school and college, and he'd always
had a particular love and affinity for it. After he finished college he joined the Peace Corps agricultural program, and he
was working in Ecuador at the time of my father's death. I
had little hope that he'd agree to come back, but it seemed, in
those white days, that anything could be tried. We talked over
crackling wires, a world away from each other; he still felt an
allegiance to the place and to my father, and he said he'd take
on the farm after his stint in the Peace Corps ended. His
agreement felt like a great simplification. At the very least it
would allow the family to get its bearings again, and to live
on in the old image for a time. It helped me to believe that
though our place here was passing, the world we'd established
might continue.

Though Dave has been running the farm for years now,
has hired his own crew, and has his own ideas for growth,
there are practical things he and I talk over still, and sometimes he asks for advice. There's much to be anxious about, as
there always has been, though I usually hold my tongue or
choose my words to frame observations rather than sugges-
tions: "Corn will never be the draw it once was . . ." I say,
fading off, walking away. I try to resist the impulse to drag
my past into his ideas for the future—"We always did it this
way." It's a bit of a joke between us. When he started some

early corn in the greenhouse one year, I laughed and said, "What's that I hear—the sound of my father turning in his grave?"

I miss the clarity you get from training an eye on the frosts and failures, from the exhaustion of working in the open air, and the way that exhaustion sharpens the wine smell of the apple cellar when it's packed to the ceiling in late fall. Over the past years I've begun to feel lighter on the land, until now I am almost a ghost when I walk across the fields to pick a few tomatoes for dinner, or pull up a corner of my shirt to collect some apples for sauce. Sometimes I watch the crew down at the far edge of a field calling to each other in Spanish as they bend to the plantings among bright yellow tubs loaded with tomatoes, squash, and cukes. A new man might stand and stare at me for a moment before narrowing his attention to the work again, but he doesn't hail me. Once when I went to find David to talk about some business and asked one of the men where he might be, he turned to another: "Where David? The lady is looking for David."

It's not the changes themselves that feel so strange—the larger scale, the different crops, the new workers. There have always been changes, and had I been part of them, I would have been swept along with them. But standing apart makes even the small changes feel significant. It can be a relief to slip into the woods at the edge of the farm, so closed in and intimate come summer. Up the dry hill beyond the brook, the moss and old nurse logs breathe their punky smell of dankness and decay. You might imagine you're walking on a moderate sea, the way the unearthed roots of old pines and the hollows they've left behind have moldered into swells and troughs beneath the duff, and fallen trunks with their whirls of limbs lie like the staves of old wrecks, half buried and fretted with the work of insects. But these woods are the abandoned far pastures from a time when farming was the common life, so you can't walk for long before your thoughts are turned inward by remnants of past labors gone to seed. A little south of the brook, just beyond an old cattle bridge, you'll come upon a forgotten orchard where trees still carry a trace of the mind and hand that shaped them, and everywhere through the woods are runs of stone walls and barbed wire, heaps of rusting metal and broken bottles, a corroding milk can with a lady fern unfurling from a lacy hole in its side. The rust and ruin, the riot of green—mutually incongruous—have created a society of their own. The rain and sun and shadow that decay one feed the other.

If you travel a few hours west, beyond the Worcester hills and the Connecticut Valley, you come to quieter, steeper country, a later frontier where cultivation has always been more difficult and tenuous than on our milder coastal terrain. Still, since there's less residential and industrial development there, the patterns of agriculture are more obvious: ancient sugar maples line the roads, and you can count an unbroken string of farmhouses one after another. As I drive through I find myself reciting the child's song: *big house, little house, back house, barn.* A few sheep graze on a slope, a herd of dairy cows lie in a pasture. Modest farmstands dot the roadsides, little more than tables stacked with tomatoes and corn, a jar for money, maybe a sign: EVERYTHING WE SELL WE GROW HERE. My family's farm looked the same fifty years ago.

In some places the woods closing in over the mantle of the hills are nearing the backs of the buildings. You can peer into the trees and see collapsed barns. When this world is released from cultivation it returns to a more northerly aspect than our own. Hemlocks and sugar maples climb the rough ledgy heights where bobcats can hide themselves. Summer people like it. There are driveways leading to new places hidden away in the woods. Young families have begun to buy up the old places for their weekends, though they have trouble keeping the fields. "Even in the last twenty years, we've lost so much open land," I heard one longtime resident complain. "The new people don't keep it clear. They start out thinking they can find some old farmer who'll mow it for free . . ."

I was there last in late August—even after years away from the demands of the farm, traveling in August still feels freeing to me—and the first apples of the year were out. I pulled into a place with no name, just a hand-lettered sign that said: AP-PLES. PEACHES. I couldn't see any outdoor work being done. Everything was still. You could tell the weaker maples would begin to turn in another week or two. I stepped down into a long, low wooden room with old white walls, cave cool, cave dark, full of benches and tables stacked with crates of apples, and the air was dense with that familiar smell. A woman alone, maybe a little older than me, was grading apples, turning each one, looking for signs of insect damage, sizing them. I knew right away by her unhurried pace that she was just helping the place out to its end. There's often a lone woman at the end.

"Smells great in here," I said.

"That's what people say. I'm here all the time, so I don't notice it anymore."

"Have you got any Gravensteins? Half a dozen?"

"Sure." We talked a little bit about them, how they make such good pies.

"You don't make cider anymore, do you?"

"No, no." Which led to talk about the crisis of a few years back when a handful of people were sickened by *E. coli* in some unpasteurized apple juice in Colorado. The word of those illnesses had been so insistent on the nightly news that everyone shied away from unpasteurized cider. Sales plummeted, the state debated putting new regulations in place to require pasteurization—untenable for small orchards that squeeze their own drops and seconds in a mill, something that a farm might depend on to make a marginal crop worthwhile.

"We'd take people down to show them how we washed the apples before we pressed them into cider," she said, "and still they were afraid to buy it. Fifty years we never had a problem and then—"

"I know, I know. I haven't had any cider since. It just doesn't taste the same."

It seemed we wanted to talk about everything, our families getting older, the fate of the farms. "Two dairy farms in town went out just last year . . . And you go over toward the river, and you see all that beautiful level, loamy farmland where you don't have to dig up the rocks, where the tractors don't tip, and you see them building houses on it."

After a while I grew a little self-conscious about interfering with her work, though she didn't seem to mind. Or maybe the discomfort I felt had to do with her devotion to the place, which seemed so assured to me, and the way she read some devotion in me. She went on, "We lost 95 percent of our crop last year."

"Oh, the frost in May—you're colder here—it must have been worse." We ran on for a while again about the apples.

"It's nice to talk to someone who knows."

"Yes, yes, it is," I said back, and I left her there, sizing and grading the Paula Reds and the Gravensteins in the deep, rich smell of the place. When I walked out I saw the brushy, unkempt edge of the fields and it was clear to me that the woods were creeping into the upper reaches of the farm, that the deer were already coming down, and the thrushes were calling out from the low places.

Often when it comes, the end of cultivation is no louder than the tumbling of apples into crates in a cave-cool, cave-dark room, but the life lived in the wake of its disappearance is a break with a long history, and the days that follow—as the worked and tended country disappears, along with its bales and stacks, rows and grids, the men and women moving among them—are different in intent and kind. It may take a while for the idea of it to die away—there may be a romanticized echo, in which farming's rewards are imagined more vividly than its costs—but its end is one of those times the whole pattern shakes and quivers and settles into new shapes and figures, perhaps all the more so in a country dependent on the idea of agriculture for its identity. In America, not only do individual dreams have their origins in farming, the notion of the Republic is stowed there as well. *Cultivators of the earth are the most valuable citizens,* insisted Thomas Jefferson. *They are the most vigorous, the most independent, the most virtuous, & they are tied to their country & wedded to it's liberty & interests by the most lasting bonds.*

On the worked-over lands of the Northeast, where the new has settled on top of the old again and again, the boundary between the smallest field and woodlands remains a kind of frontier. Or perhaps it's more accurate to think of it as a contour of human time—it's always a question of time: how much to acquiesce and try to inhabit its flow, how much to try to make a mark against it, how much heed to give to the past attempts everywhere evident on the land. If you have maintained such a boundary all your life and you see a little brush growing into the clearing, you can get a creeping feeling at the back of your neck. You understand how small your own enterprise is, and how temporary. *That's what I despise—brush and trees growing in hay fields,* remarked one farmer early in the twentieth century. I've been startled to hear another insist: "I'd rather see a hundred houses in my fields than have the woods come back on it."

The woods *have* come back on it even where agriculture hasn't been entirely lost. As New England dairy herds were sold and farmers turned more frequently to market garden cultivation, the rougher pastures were let go. My family's farm, in the years I've known it, contains much less cleared land than it had in 1901. Today the row crops, the corn and tomatoes and peppers and beans, are concentrated on the most productive land. Without adjoining farms, and only a few others scattered among suburban tracts, ours is smaller within the community as well, though in some strange way it is also more prominent now that farming is no longer the common life.

Though the margin between our cleared land and woods remains certain for now, I can't help feeling the farm may be swallowed up soon, and a whole world will go with it, one that has been both particular to ourselves and representative of the many who have contended with the land and brought their histories to bear upon it. As if understanding can alleviate loss, I am trying to place our own time within the larger story of cultivation. I hope constraint amplifies, that by giving shape to the stories, to the persistent half-lives of the vanished who roam even on stinging winter days, I can see more clearly where we belong in the accumulation of beliefs, ideas, violence, necessities, and desires that have determined this country. But the beginnings *are* hazy, and the people there seem so different. The moment I try to articulate something of the story, which is its own attempt at defining a frontier once and for all, the boundaries seem to change again. Even as I write this down now my understanding clears and grows back in, clears and grows back in, and I know if I let go, if I turn my back on it even for a little bit, I'll have to remake it out of the rank that has grown back. The stories flux like fall migrations, forming and re-forming, part of them gaining as another part recedes, the labor of it continuous, and still the lines dream their own way, on the wind.

AGRICULTURAL TIME

The earliest depiction I've seen of fields on these shores are the eight stands of ripening corn sketched on Samuel de Champlain's 1605 map of what he called Port St. Louis. The place was later established as the settlement of Plymouth, but on Champlain's map smoke rises from wigwams in the Wampanoag village of Patuxet, leafy trees are scattered along the shore, and dense forest crowds spits of land at either end of the harbor. Depth soundings—1, 2, 8, 9, 10—are plotted on the water. How long Patuxet had existed before that map I can't know, but it wasn't to last much longer. An epidemic in 1617 killed two-thirds of the Indian inhabitants of the region: thousands lay dead in and around their wigwams, so many that the living were unable to bury them, and their bones were bleached by the sun. The disease wiped out the village almost entirely. Squanto, the one survivor, had been sold into slavery in Europe and avoided death by being absent. After his eventual escape and improbable journey back to his own shore, he found his home deserted.

By the time the *Mayflower* anchored in the harbor in December 1620, the fields Champlain had drawn were rank with weeds. William Bradford's account of the settlement at Plymouth makes no mention of the disease, or of wigwams. *They sounded the harbor and found it fit for shipping, and marched into the land and found divers cornfields and little running brooks, a place (as they supposed) fit for situation,* he wrote. *At least it was the best they could find, and the season and their present necessity made them glad to accept of it.*

Within days the Pilgrims began building rudimentary shelters; within months they'd made a treaty with Massasoit, chief of the Wampanoag, who'd agreed:

1. *That neither he nor any of his should injure or do hurt to any of their people.*
2. *That if any of his did hurt to any of theirs, he should send the offender, that they might punish him.*
3. *That if anything were taken away from any of theirs, he should cause it to be restored; and they should do the like to his.*
4. *If any did unjustly war against him, they would aid him; if any did war against them, he should aid them.*
5. *He should send to his neighbours confederates to certify them of this, that they might not wrong them, but might be likewise comprised in the conditions of peace.*
6. *That when their men came to them, they should leave their bows and arrows behind them.*

However detailed the words, the treaty never did allay the apprehensions of the colonists. William Bradford continued to see the Algonquin as skulkers at the borders: in the pages after the recording of the treaty he writes of the killing of some settlers, and for him it stood as proof of *how far these people were from peace, and with what danger this plantation was begun, save as the powerful hand of the Lord did protect them.*

All the while the winter took its toll on the colony. Only one of the Pilgrims had perished during the crossing, yet in those first months at Plymouth sometimes two or three a day would die of hunger, cold, or disease: *. . . of 100 and odd persons, scarce fifty remained,* wrote Bradford. *And of these, in the time of most distress, there was but six or seven sound persons who . . . fetched them wood, made them fires, dressed them meat, made their beds, washed their loathsome clothes, clothed and unclothed them.* By the time the frost was out of the ground only twenty-one men and six grown boys were strong enough to prepare the fields for planting, and they could hardly be called farmers. Most had been involved in the clothing industry in Holland. William Brewster had been a village postmaster; John Carver, a businessman; Edward Winslow, a printer; Myles Standish, a soldier. They had few adequate tools. No oxen or plows are listed on the *Mayflower* bill of lading.

They would not have survived without those fields at Patuxet, which saved them the labor of clearing land for planting, and the ten bushels of stored Indian flint corn the Pilgrims had unearthed during their explorations of Cape Cod prior to settlement at Plymouth, and Squanto, who *stood them in great stead, showing them both the manner how to set [corn], and after how to dress and tend it. Also he told them, except they got fish and set with it in these old grounds it would come to nothing . . . and taught them how to take it, and where to get other provisions necessary for them. All which they found true by trial and experience. Some English seed they sowed, as wheat and pease, but it came not to good, either by the badness of the seed or lateness of the season, or both, or some other defect.*

The land they'd cultivated in Plymouth was not only the best they could find, it was about as good as it would get for farming. *The soil is for general a warm kind of earth,* wrote William Wood in his *New England's Prospect* in 1634, *there being little cold spewing land, no moorish fens, no quagmires . . . Such is the rankness of the ground that it must be sown the first year with Indian corn, which is a soaking grain, before it will be fit to receive English seed. In a word, as there is no ground so purely good as the long forced and improved grounds of England, so is there none so extremely bad as in many places of England that as yet have not been manured and improved . . . Wherefore it is neither impossible, nor much improbable, that upon improvements the soil may be as good in time as England.*

But New England soil has always had its own demands. It's largely an inconsistent swirl of glacial till—often rock-strewn, acidic, and quick to lose its fertility. *We found after five or six years that it grows barren beyond belief,* one colonist would comment early on. The Wampanoag, like other Algonquin, had cleared and planted such lands without oxen, iron, or knowledge of the wheel. Their tools were made of shell and wood, stone and bone, and were useful only on light, well-drained soils that could be turned up with the shoulder bones of deer. Of necessity, then, they left the heavy lands and clay soils untouched, keeping their cultivations to the gentle hilltops, the south-facing slopes that warm up early, the richer soils in the intervales, the clearings along the coast. To make new fields they burned stands of white pine, which thrive on lighter soils. The softwood could be felled with a stone ax, and fire—helped by resin and dry needles—would work fast. Fire once to burn the brush, fire twice to burn the trunks, and again to make a cindery bed. They grew beans and squash, but their mainstay was flint corn, which they beat into meal and sifted through a basket. Sometimes they parched it, or wrapped the cornmeal in leaves and baked it in ashes, or made small cakes and boiled them.

Since the Algonquin supplemented their cultivated stores with wild meat, berries, plants, and acorns from the surrounding woodlands, they burned the underbrush in some of the forested areas for easier hunting and gathering. In winter they moved their villages inland, away from the bitter ocean winds, and returned to the coast in summer to fish, and to plant in the milder season there. They kept no livestock, so they had no need to raise extensive fields of grasses for feed and fodder. Their compact and movable life, shoaling between woodlands and cultivations, created a pattern on the land close to the drift of the soils with their runs and swirls and settlings. It bewildered English eyes, which were long accustomed to determined villages and an ordered, patchwork landscape. *The Indians are not able to make use of one fourth part of the land,* one observer insisted, *neither have they any settled places, as towns, to dwell in; nor any ground as they challenge for their own possession, but change their habitation from place to place.*

In much of England and central Europe you'd have had to go back to the ninth and tenth centuries to find a world that depended on only lighter soils for cultivation. Few in the seventeenth century would have had any memory of the incremental clearing of the land, or the initial plowing of fields, of the slow evolution of cart tracks into strong roads as villages became established and trade routes and market days flourished. Drainage systems had, by then, obscured old bounds. Horses plowed established fields quickly while oxen reclaimed heavier lands from the wild, clearing more and more efficiently as collars and yokes became sturdier, and plows stronger. Populations had grown and had become more mobile in the increasing stability. More horses, cattle, oxen, and workers required more acreage in wheat and oats, barley and rye.

By the seventeenth century there had long existed written instruction on how to keep oxen and how to inspect cattle. Documents dating back to the Middle Ages listed expected yields of grain, and instructed farmers on how to feed the dung heap, how to fertilize and rotate crops. The character of those who work the soil had also been set down: *The plough-men ought to be men of intelligence, and ought to know how to sow, and how to repair and mend broken ploughs and har-rows, and to till the land well, and crop it rightly; and they ought to know also how to yoke and drive the oxen, without beating or hurting them . . . And they and the keepers must make ditches, and build and remove the earth . . .* Such an idea of the cultivator isn't so far from Plato's description of the farmers of prehistoric Athens, *a class of genuine full-time agriculturists with good natural talents and high standards.*

Plato compared that legendary Athens to the one of his own time. The fertile lands and careful practices of former days lived large in memory, and seemed to chasten his present:

. . . the rich, soft soil has all run away leaving the land nothing but skin and bone. But in those days the damage had not taken place, the hills had high crests, the rocky plain of Phelleus was covered with rich soil, and the mountains were covered by thick woods, of which there are some traces today. For some mountains which today will only support bees produced not so long ago trees which when cut provided roof beams for huge buildings whose roofs are still standing. And there were a lot of tall cultivated trees which bore unlimited quantities of fodder for beasts. The soil benefited from an annual rainfall which did not run to waste off the bare earth as it does today . . .

The past, with its own power and life, imbues all kinds of land. Sometimes an idea is born of erosions. René Dubos would speculate on the damaged lands of Greece, the white rocks and the sun-loving aromatic plants—the idea of Greece that has grown in our own minds: *I have wondered whether the dark and ferocious divinities of the preclassical Greek period did not become more serene and more playful precisely because they had emerged from the dark forest into the open landscape. Would logic have flourished if Greece had remained covered with an opaque tangle of trees?*

Would our sense of a patchwork agricultural world as a proper country have flourished if seventeenth-century Europe hadn't long lost its tangle of trees? Woodlands had grown scarce by then because of the increased clearing of fields and the constant demand for wood. Wood was needed for housing and fuel, for masts and hulls of ships, to make casks, vats, and vine props for vineyards, to produce resin for torches, bark for rope makers, ash, and charcoal. Strict rules concerning the felling of trees had been set down. *Every one of our commune shall be bound to plant each year ten domestic trees . . . Let no one dare to cut larchpoles to make firewood on this mountain . . . Let no one dare to cut wood from Xomo up to the rock of Slamer and from the peak of the mountains towards Xomo, save to construct a house or for the fire, on pain of five sous per tree.*

I've wondered where the idea of wilderness goes when the woods disappear, the woods that had sheltered beggars and hid salt smugglers and thieves, that—however frightening—had also been useful to men and women bound by a feudal system which, no matter how much they worked, left them begging at the gates of the rich come winter. They could turn their animals out to feed on beech mast, they could gather mushrooms, berries, and herbs to appease their hunger. The mystery of the indifferent and necessary woodlands could not be distinguished from its terrors, the many terrors could not be distinguished one from the other.

As cultivation progressed and forests diminished, and as both European villagers and farmers came to rely more on cultivation and less and less on foraging in the dwindling woodlands for their survival, I imagine that what wilderness remained became more daunting—less of a refuge, less complex in people's understanding, so that by the seventeenth century, when Europe was largely a cultivated landscape, the woodlands had become incomprehensible. When the first white settlers were confronted with the extensive eastern forests of the New World, however much they may have been burned and cultivated by the Wampanoag, Nipmuck, and others, they couldn't see a way through, and marveled at the way the Indians could: *A man may travel many days and*

*never find [a path. The Indian, however,] sees it instantly . . .
and will mark his courses as he runs more readily than most
Travellers who steer by the Compass.*

In the first years of settlement the colonists at Plymouth kept
their plantings tight within an impaled world—in part for the
protection it offered from the Indian tribes and from everything they understood as wilderness, but also out of necessity. The work had to be done communally—they hadn't the
strength to cultivate large swaths individually. As well, they
were obliged to work together to send quantities of clapboard, fur, and sassafras to their backers in England. Only after several years of settlement, after the constraints imposed
by their backers lessened, and their desires for their own lives
had room to grow, was each colonist granted a modest plot.
William Bradford remembers: *And to every person was given
only one acre of land, to them and theirs, as near the town as
might be . . . The reason was that they might be kept close together, both for more safety and defense, and the better im-
provement of the general employments. Which condition of
theirs did make me often think of what I had read in Pliny of
the Romans' first beginnings in Romulus's time. How every
man contented himself with two acres of land, and had no
more assigned them . . . And long after, the greatest present
given to a Captain that had got a victory over their enemies,
was as much ground as they could till in one day. And he was
not counted a good, but a dangerous man, that would not
content himself with seven acres of land.*

As the colonists became more secure in the New World,
the varieties and amounts of crops they grew increased. They
planted root crops of English origin such as turnips, parsnips,

and onions alongside the wheat and barley they had been cultivating from the start, and *they began now highly to prize corn as more precious than silver.* In addition, they were raising livestock, which required extensive fields and pasture. Each family necessarily required more land for planting and grazing, and Bradford details the way in which the bounds of the community were loosened: *For now as their stocks increased, and the increase vendible, there was no longer anything holding them together, but now they must of necessity go to their own great lots. They could not otherwise keep their cattle, and having oxen grown they must have land for plowing and tillage. And no man now thought he could live except he had cattle and a great deal of ground to keep them, all striving to increase their stocks. By which means they were scattered all over the Bay quickly and the town, in which they had lived compactly till now was left very thin and in a short time almost desolate.*

More expansion rapidly followed. By 1638, less than twenty years after the settlement began, Plymouth Colony consisted of 356 fields covering five square miles, and a considerable number of other towns had established themselves along the coast and up the rivers, natural places for settlement since they afforded travel by water—few roads reached into the interior—and colonists could avail themselves of nearby wild grasslands.

Europeans had long depended on cultivated grasses such as timothy and redtop to feed their livestock. Such grasses weren't native to the New World, and weren't to become es-

tablished until early in the 1700s, after timothy was discovered growing in New Hampshire, having sown itself there, it
is supposed, from seeds carried over in the bedding and ballast of ships. But in the first years of settlement, fresh meadows along the rivers and, more important, the vast salt grass
marshlands along the sandy shores of the coast—vaster than
anything imaginable now that so many of them have been
ditched and drained—stood in for the calm and order of English fields, and were essential to colonial survival. They were
time given, since wild grasses served as a ready crop on land
farmers didn't need to clear or tend. Men could harvest feed
for their livestock and turn to their other concerns. *There is so
much hay ground in the country as the richest voyagers that
shall venture thither need not fear want of fodder, though his
herd increase into thousands, there being thousands of acres
that yet was never meddled with,* William Wood was to comment. *True it is that it is not so fine to the eye as English grass,
but it is not sour, though it grow thus rank, but being made
into hay the cattle eat it as well as it were lea hay and like as
well with it.*

The salt marshes really are no more than built-up detritus:
season after season of thatch and stubble and the wash and
drift that gets caught in roots and stalks, earth made of soft
spots, little mires, marsh pools, peat and pan, smelling of low
tide, of dead sea life and brine. *Spartina alterniflora*, a crude
grass that's heavy enough to be used for the thatch on houses,
defines the open edges of the marshlands. If you nose in with
your kayak on a clear summer day, you can see the salt
glinting on its stalks. Come winter the ice cuts the withered
grasses, and as they mat and decay they build up the earth
into solid enough ground for *Spartina patens*—a finer grass,

most prized for salt hay—to establish itself. The grasses possess a complex set of adaptations that enable them to exclude and excrete much of the salt in seawater in order to survive on the tidal marshes. It's not that they necessarily thrive there— they'd grow larger and contain more nutritive value on higher, fresher ground—but spartina can't successfully compete with other plants in an inland meadow, and so it keeps its place on the sea-laden edge of land where little else can grow. No, salt hay could never be confused with English hay. Sea pickle and warts and sea lavender grow among it, dead crabs and wrack get caught in the stalks. It brought the smell of the sea into colonial barns and bedding and households. Heavy and crude, it didn't scatter on the wind like cut timothy. It served as fodder but wouldn't fatten the cattle. An experienced colonial farmer, less optimistic than Wood, complained: *Our beasts grow lousy with feeding upon it and are much out of heart and liking.*

The salt hay harvest began in late summer, during the spring tide, just when the waters had ebbed and the stalks of grass were still moist for cutting. On farms bordering the marshes, the men might work together to get in the harvest. They'd cut the spartina and the adjacent black grass on the higher grounds through September until the frost, and sometimes after the frost, though what was harvested then was used for banking houses rather than for fodder, since once the hay froze it lost its value as feed. *[They] took scythes out to mow the marsh in August when the grass was tall but not yet mature . . . The men moved along, three abreast, and cut the high marsh grasses. After the hay was cured the men gathered it by pitchfork and piled it into stacks . . . On the lower reaches sure to be flooded, the salt hay was cut and carried to the upland, perhaps to be put in the barn. On the high marsh, the hay was piled on small poles driven into the surface of the soil in clusters about two feet high and two feet apart. On these groups of small pilings, called staddles, the hay was safe from high tides. The hay was collected in the fall if necessary, but usually it was left until winter came and the frozen marsh surface could support an ox team and sledge . . . Sometimes an unusually high tide occurred when a regular high was made higher by strong winds in an autumn storm. Then the carefully piled haystacks floated off the staddles intact and finally lodged up against the land somewhere . . .*

The dependency on those marshes was to diminish once colonists established fields of English hay on inland grounds, but the distinction between wild grasses and cultivated ones lived on in the imagination. *Rise free from care before dawn, and seek adventures,* instructed Thoreau in the nineteenth century. *Let the noon find thee by other lakes, and night overtake thee every where at home. There are no larger fields than these, no worthier games than may here be played. Grow wild according to thy nature, like these sedges and brakes, which will never become English hay.* When Thoreau made his comparison between wild and tame lives, agriculture had already begun its decline in New England. The cultivated bordered the abandoned; the ceaseless effort of farming was thrown up against itself. No wonder he would free the human spirit from the demands of the field: *Let the thunder rumble; what if it threaten ruin to farmers crops? that is not its errand to thee. Take shelter under the cloud, while they flee to carts and sheds . . . Men come tamely home at night only from the next field or street, where their household echoes haunt and their life pines because it breathes its own breath over and over again; their shadows morning and evening reach farther than their daily steps.*

When I look at the salt marshes now I see in the planes of field and sea and sky a place apparently washed of human effort—you would never imagine a workday as you gaze at them, or how they once defined a world and allowed it to continue. Sometimes kayaks and other small craft course through the meanders, but otherwise few humans enter the marshes, and to do so feels almost forbidden. Spare and quiet, soothing, fetid, contemplative, they now feel like the most solitary part of our crowded, overbuilt section of New England. An egret stalks its prey, the grasses cowl and whisper in a storyless world, seabirds cry overhead—always closer to a keening than a song.

Fenced-in fields distinguished the settled world more clearly from disordered nature, and also from the less distinctive clearings and movable villages of the Algonquin. The colonists were never to regard Indian villages as land possessed—*As for the Natiues in New England, they inclose no Land,* noted Roger Williams, *neither haue any setled habytation, nor any tame Cattle to proue the Land by*—and they persistently expanded onto Indian lands. The Wampanoag, Nipmuck, and other eastern Massachusetts tribes were vexed by cattle trampling their cornfields and their clam beds, and they were pushed farther and farther back from the coast and the river valleys, from the light soils they had cleared and planted. *You have driven us out of our own Countrie and then pursued us to our Great Miserie, and Your own, and we are Forced to live upon you,* one Indian was to claim. The colonists were not only arriving in unimagined numbers and claiming extensive lands, they were following the Algonquin patterns of settlement along the coast and up the rivers. On Cape Cod and the south coast of Massachusetts: Plymouth, Sandwich, Eastham, Harwich, Yarmouth, Barnstable, Dartmouth, Taunton, Rehoboth; along what is now the Rhode Island coast: Providence and Warwick; the north shore of Massachusetts and up the Merrimack River: Gloucester, Ipswich, Newbury, Amesbury, Salisbury, Haverhill . . . Like Plymouth itself, all these towns—almost every early New England town—had at their hearts an Algonquin field.

With each colonial push for new settlement, the fragile peace that had been established between Massasoit and Plymouth Colony in those first months of the first year frayed more. In 1675 Massasoit's son, Philip, embarked on what is known as King Philip's War, which still stands as the bloodiest per capita in the history of the country. Indian attacks on established colonial villages destroyed lives, cattle, crops, and houses. *Though English man hath provoked us to anger & wrath & we care not though we have war with you this 21 years for there are many of us 300 hundred of which hath fought with you at this town[.] we hauve nothing but our lives to loose but thou has many fair houses cattell & much good things,* reads the note a retreating Indian tacked to a tree as the town of Medfield burned. And another elsewhere: *You know, and we know, you have great sorrowful with crying; for you lost many, many hundred men, and all your house, all your land, and woman, child, and cattle, and all your things that you have lost.*

As Jill Lepore observes in *The Name of War,* by destroying

colonial possessions the Algonquin undermined the idea of the world the colonists carried with them, and had striven to apply to new land: *Colonial writers understood the destruction of houses as a blow not only to their property but also to the very Englishness of the landscape . . . Nearly all of the damage to the English during King Philip's War—the burning of houses, the spilling of blood . . . —was understood as attacks on bounded systems. While disorder threatened to rule New England, military strategists sought means to draw a line to keep Indians—and chaos—out. In Massachusetts, alarmed colonists even debated building an eight-foot-high wall of stone or wood all the way from the Charles River to the bay, "by which meanes that whole tract will [be] environed for the security & safety (under God) of the people, their houses, goods & cattel; from the rage & fury of the enimy."*

After a year of war, the bounded world of the colonists was almost completely destroyed: *In Narraganset, not one House left standing. At Warwick, but one. At Providence, not above three . . . Marlborough, wholy laid in Ashes, except two or three Houses . . . Many Houses burnt at Springfield, Scituate, Lancaster, Brookefield, and Northampton. The greatest Part of Rehoboth and Taunton destroyed. Great spoil made at Hadley, Hatfield, and Chelmsford. Deerfield wholly, and Westfield much ruined . . . Besides particular Farms and Plantations, a great Number not to be reckoned up, wholly laid waste, or much damnified.*

If the Algonquin had only their lives to lose, it was their lives they lost. Nearly all the Christian Indians who had been captured and imprisoned on Deer Island in Boston Harbor starved to death during the winter of the war. Most of those along the coast who weren't killed were sold into slavery; a remnant were squeezed west against their longtime adversaries, the Mohawks.

Savage on both sides, exhausting and debilitating, the war never had an official end—skirmishes were to continue for years—and a vehemence regarding the Indians remained stubbornly coiled in the colonial mind, evidenced in the way Philip's remains were treated. In August 1676 he was cornered in a swamp near his home territory of Mount Hope. After he was shot dead he was beheaded and quartered. His attackers took his head to Plymouth and mounted it on a pole—*meat to the people inhabiting the wilderness*, Increase Mather was to say—where it was to remain even as Philip's cornfields were sold to a Boston businessman and the new owner began to raise and export onions to England, as English settlement pushed inland far beyond the light soils of the Algonquin fields, as new settlers made cropland out of rich soils beneath the sugar maple and beech forests, and made pasture out of the fair soils beneath the chestnut and oak in the uplands, as colonists cut enormous quantities of wood for fences, houses, fuel for fires, boxes, barrels, as wood was piled and burned, or sent to the sawmills until only the wet and rocky ground of hemlock and red maple remained forested. Years after Philip's death, Increase's son, Cotton Mather, journeyed to Plymouth to gaze upon what remained of the head and he *took off the Jaw from the Blasphemous exposed Skull of that Leviathan.*

As colonial settlers inched westward and northward, their fields, though they may have been more marked and orderly than those of the Algonquin, were still fundamen-

tally different from the long-established European fields of
their memories, imaginations, and initial expectations. Where
they'd ventured beyond the already-tilled light soils of the Algonquin and the natural grasslands along the waterways to
make farmland out of the wild, inevitably the initial clearing
of such land was disorderly and rough, with uprootings and
slash, exposed soils and downed trunks. Colonists might
spend the fall of one year cutting and burning a woodland,
and the following spring plant their first crop—squash, beans,
barley, corn, onions—among the stumps and char. In most
places the soil would have been scattered with stones, the glacial debris which was always to define and limit New England
agriculture. To visiting Europeans familiar only with cultivation on long-established fields, this process of making land
out of the wild was bewildering. Upon seeing America for the
first time, one visitor wrote: *The scene is truly savage, immense trees stripped of their foliage, and half consumed by
fire extend their sprawling limbs, the parts of which untouched by the fire, now bleached by the weather, form a
stronger contrast with the charring of the remainder; the
ground is strewn with immense stones, many of them a size
far too large to be movable, interspersed with the stumps of
the lesser trees which have been cut off about a yard from the
ground.*

Colonists continued to make new fields out of the wild in
part because of increased settlement, but also because the
sheer abundance of available land seemed to discourage pru-
dent agricultural practices. European cultivation, having depended on a gradual progression of technologies, had grown
slowly and methodically. In its early stages the rudimentary
nature of the tools and the scarcity of work animals was to

limit how much land could be cleared, and how quickly such clearing could be accomplished. Difficulty promoted care. Not for nothing was the plowman deemed exemplary who would work *to till the land well, and crop it rightly* so as to maintain fertility. Even later, after much of the countryside was cleared, European cultivation continued to be one of limits. Prior to the discovery of the New World, with its seemingly endless possibilities for expansion, Europeans understood that to support the growing population of their continent they necessarily had to maintain the fertility of their soils.

Once the initial fertility of the soil is lost, it is difficult to regain, but agricultural practices that maintain fertility are extremely labor-intensive—especially without the aid of modern fertilizers and machines—and in the colonial world would have involved the care of the dung heap, the spreading of manure, the planning that goes into crop rotation. In the New World, with so much available land to carve into—and to be ordered—if after a few years' time the vitality of the soil diminished, sometimes it was easier for a settler to cut a new field than to take time to manage the old one, to worry about fertilizing and rotating crops. The abandoned field, without trees or cultivation to hold it, would be subject to erosion. Once topsoil, the product of millions of years of weather and decay and buildup, was lost, it could not be recovered. Land no longer productive would be abandoned to the wild once again.

As the distinction between the old ideas of Europe and new realities of America grew more pronounced, the distinctiveness of the American farmer became something increasingly articulated, and increasingly complex, an argument with itself, with the wild, with the Europe left behind. In the later eighteenth century in J. Hector St. John de Crèvecœur's *Letters from an American Farmer*, his Farmer James would write to a French correspondent suggesting the first clearers of land were one particular kind of American: *He, who would wish to see America in its proper light, and to have a true idea of its feeble beginnings and barbarous rudiments, must visit our extended line of frontiers, where the last settlers dwell, and where he may see the first labours of settlement, the mode of clearing the earth, in all their different appearances . . . By living in or near the woods, their actions are regulated by the wildness of the neighbourhood. The deer often come to eat their grain, the wolves to destroy their sheep, the bears to kill their hogs, the foxes to catch their poultry. This surrounding hostility immediately puts the gun into their hands . . . Once hunters, farewel to the plough. The chase renders them ferocious, gloomy, and unsocial . . . These new manners, being grafted on old stock, produce a strange sort of lawless profligacy, the impressions of which are indelible. The manners of the Indian natives are respectable compared with this European medley . . . Thus are our first steps trodden, thus are our first trees felled, in general, by the most vicious of our people.*

Those who farmed in the settlers' wake were another kind of American, Crèvecœur believed, at once closer in kind to the cultivators of the squarely cleared fields of Europe, but distinguished from the European farmer by dint of possession: *and thus the path is opened for the arrival of a second and better class, the true American freeholders; the most respectable set of people in this part of the world: respectable for their industry, their happy independence, the great share of freedom they possess . . . Here nature opens her broad lap to receive the perpetual accession of new comers, and to supply them with food . . . Here we have, in some measure, regained the ancient dignity of our species; our laws are simple and just; we are a race of cultivators; our cultivation is unrestrained, and therefore everything is prosperous and flourishing . . . The instant I enter on my own land, the bright idea of property, of exclusive right of independence, exalt my mind. Precious soil, I say to myself . . . What should we American farmers be without the distinct possession of that soil?*

But cultivation's hold is always tenuous. The sense of order and safety it imparts will change if you turn your back on it: the brush grows in, the night comes on, old fears crowd you. It's a skittering truth—if it is a truth at all—and in danger of unimagined outside forces taking it away. Even the seeming certain world of Crèvecœur's true freeholder could be turned on its head by a change of fortune. By his twelfth and final letter, the American Revolution had begun, and Farmer James was writing out of a war-torn world. *I wish for a change of place,* his last letter begins, *the hour is come at last that I must fly from my house and abandon my farm! But what course shall I steer, inclosed as I am? . . . The property of farmers is not like that of merchants . . . my former respect, my former attachment vanishes with my safety . . . since I have ceased to consider myself as a member of the ancient state, now convulsed, I willingly descend into an inferior one. I will revert into a state approaching nearer to that of nature . . .* In the midst of war's destruction and its necessary realignments, he allied himself with a life lifted out of an old order, perhaps as only one without experience of the wild could dream and mythologize it: *Thus shall we metamorphose our-*

*selves, from neat, decent, opulent, planters, surrounded with
every conveniency which our external labour and internal industry could give, into a still simpler people divested of every
thing beside hope, food, and the raiment of the woods: abandoning the large framed house, to dwell under the wigwham;
and the feather-bed, to lie on the mat or bear's skin. There
shall we sleep undisturbed by frightful dreams and apprehensions; rest and peace of mind will make us the most ample
amends for what we shall leave behind.*

Perhaps no one more than Thomas Jefferson was to keep
turning the idea of the cultivator over in his mind, refining
it and redefining it as the nation changed and expanded.
Jefferson understood the farmer to be the true citizen of the
Republic: *Those who labour in the earth are the chosen
people of God, if ever he had a chosen people, whose breasts
he has made his peculiar deposit for substantial and genuine
virtue. It is the focus in which he keeps alive that sacred
fire, which otherwise might escape from the face of the earth.*
And possession of the land was essential to the character
of the farmer. He would exhort the Cherokee: *You are becoming farmers, learning the use of the plough and the hoe,
enclosing your grounds and employing that labor in their
cultivation which you formerly employed in hunting and
in war . . . When a man has property, earned by his own
labor, he will not like another to come and take it from
him . . .*

As Jefferson had imagined cultivators, they would not be
subsistence farmers but a liberally educated people free of ex-

cessive needs and wants who would make their clothing from their own wool and flax, who'd produce their own food and raise a surplus for export, so that there would be no need to depend on manufacturing for wealth. By encouraging a society of farmers, he had hopes of avoiding what he saw as the fate of Europe: nations living down through time, and hampered by decay, whose countrysides had suffered from farmers striking their hoes into rented fields, and others turning away from the land to work in factories. He writes from Nice, France: *I have been pleased to find among the people a less degree of physical misery than I had expected. They are generally well clothed, and have plenty of food, not animal indeed, but vegetable, which is as wholesome. Perhaps they are over worked, the excess of the rent required by the landlord, obliging them to too many hours of labor, in order to produce that, and wherewith to feed and clothe themselves. The soil of Champagne and Burgundy I have found more universally good than I had expected, and as I could not help making a comparison with England, I found that comparison more unfavorable to the latter than is generally admitted. The soil, the climate, and the production are superior to those of England and the husbandry as good, except one point; that of manure . . . Here the leases are either during pleasure, or for three, six, or nine years, which does not give the farmer time to repay himself for the expensive operation of well manuring, and therefore, he manures ill, or not at all.*

Jefferson himself may have struggled with debt, with the erosion of his Virginia soils, and failing fertility. Like all farmers, he was at the mercy of the soil and weather, but also like all farmers nearly in the same breath he would voice satisfaction with the first ripening crops:

May 4.   *the blue ridge of mountains covered with*
            snow.
    5.   *a frost which destroyed almost every thing. it*
            killed the wheat, rye, corn, many tobacco
            plants, and even large saplings. the leaves of
            the trees were entirely killed. all the shoots of
            vines. at Monticello near half the fruit of
            every kind was killed; and before this no in-
            stance had ever occurred of any fruit killed
            here by the frost . . .
  14.   *cherries ripe.*
  16.   *first dish of pease from earliest patch.*
  26.   *a second patch of peas come to table.*

Still, his was a philosophy of farming laid out by a states-
man who had traveled the world searching for varieties of
seed that he could breed and crossbreed, who had slaves to till
his soil and international acquaintances to correspond with
about the idea of the cultivator. His desire was sometimes
freed from necessity. I can't read his *Farm and Garden Books*
with one after another entry of exotics—vines from Burgundy
and the Cape of Good Hope, African early peas, pumpkins
from South America and Malta, Italian peaches from Mazzei,
sweet almonds from Cadiz, pear cuttings from Gallipolis—
without thinking of the spare accountings my father left behind, which I'd found in the days after he'd died. My father's
farm book advises: *An annual Farm Inventory will . . . show*
your Net Worth above all debts . . . show whether or not you
are getting ahead financially and by how much. In his first
year of running the farm everything was assiduously recorded:
the 1928 Dodge and the 1926 Dodge, the manure spreaders

and harrows and cultivators, the outbuildings. Every cow, horse, and hen was accounted for. In his earnest accountings farming seems to stand apart from all philosophies and ideas. It is the names of the herd that strike me—the plainness of the names, the absence of flourish: *Cattle: Brown Swiss, Little White, Big White, Mule Ears, Long Legs, Old Jersey, Little Pure Bred, Big Pure Bred, 1/2 sister Hybred, Wisconsin Pure Bred, Horned Gurnsey . . . ; Calves: 3; Bulls: Alec; Horses, work: Big Dan, Little Dan . . .*

You can't always explain how or why an aperture opens, how you fall into a larger seeing, but reading those names, in his hand, after he had gone, was the first time I believe I truly understood how far he'd traveled in his life, and how much I had taken everything—most of all a feeling of security—for granted. I felt a little shame: all of a sudden I saw the deep hard work of it, the aspiration to be gotten bit by bit. I saw the luxury of my own dreaming mind. Maybe I'd been so late in coming to that understanding because the father I'd always known had gained some leeway—he'd been able to extend the farm by buying some of the surrounding land—and with that leeway came a sense of security, and of dominion. He had tried growing a fig tree, walnuts, champagne grapes. The same land plowed for so long out of necessity may have been working its way toward desire. Still, if you were to ask him why he farmed, he'd simply say he liked to see things grow.

For Jefferson, if the cultivators of the earth were to be eternal and the country was to grow, there would always have to be a frontier, new lands where new farmers could stream beyond original settlements and keep pushing across space, up against the Appalachians, then beyond into the backlands. If there was always a frontier, then the country could always be young with fencing and cropland and cattle defining a western border again and again, each place made by one man and one woman, again pulling up stumps and plowing earth, now with their forty acres—for forty acres was by then considered the necessary amount of land to support a family—their cultivated rows and their fenced-in cattle, the geese, the ducks, the hens, their bleaching fields, and spinning wheels. *I think our governments will remain virtuous for many centuries; as long as they are chiefly agricultural; and this will be as long as there shall be vacant lands in any part of America,* Jefferson wrote. *When they get piled upon one another in large cities, as in Europe, they will become corrupt as in Europe.* A nation of farmers would keep manufacturing at bay, but the new territory they moved into would contain the troubles of the nation: Jefferson would not oppose the expansion of slavery into the new territories, or the injustices of the acquisition of new territories through skirmishes and war. *There are but two means of acquiring the native title,* he wrote. *First, war; for even war may, sometimes, give a just title. Second, contracts or treaty.*

The heart of the New World had its own name: *prairie.* The long open center of the word conjures an endless, calm, undefined expanse, which would have stood in contrast to Jefferson's Monticello, bounded by far mountains and framed by the ascending wild: *Of prospect I have a rich profusion and offering itself at every point of the compass,* Jefferson wrote of his home. *Mountains distant & near, smooth & shaggy, single & in ridges, a little river hiding itself among the hills so as to shew in lagoons only, cultivated grounds under the eye and two small villages. To prevent a satiety of this is the prin-cipal difficulty. It may be successively offered, & in different proportions through vistas, or which will be better, between thickets so disposed as to serve as vistas, with the advantage of shifting the scenes as you advance on your way.* But to play out his dream for a whole country, to democratize it, what could be more perfect than one enormous field to be divided into individual great lots?

The first prairie the settlers encountered was the tallgrass prairie, and what it contained can seem countless: cordgrass, switchgrass, Junegrass, wild rye, milkweed, musk thistle, blue false indigo, sagewort, speedwell, sedge, sumac, watercress, yarrow, wild parsley, plum, wild strawberry, white prairie-clover, wild onion. But it was defined by big bluestem, *Andro-pogon gerardii*, which in favorable conditions grows to almost twice human height, and can endure fire, drought, and extensive grazing since most of its mass is below ground: a mat of roots sometimes twelve feet deep, thickening into a deep and rich sod so dense other species have a difficult time thriving among it. It spreads by rhizomes, and needn't depend on scattering its seed to reproduce. After the dust bowl, after the rains finally came, it was big bluestem that recovered first. When you were in it, it was said that the only direction you could see was straight up. To find grazing cattle you had to stand up in the saddle and look for movement in the grass. When weather came over the mountains from the west it brought lightning-stoked fires, and once a fire started on the prairie, the carpetlike growth ensured it would burn for a long time. One pioneer noted: *The last 12 miles we travelled after sundown and by fire light over the Prairie, it being on fire. This was the grandest scene I ever saw . . . We had a view at one time from one to 5 miles of fire in a streak, burning from 2 to 6 feet high. In high grass it sometimes burns 30 feet high, if driven by fierce winds. By the light of this fire we could read fine print for a 1/2 mile or more . . . Till I saw this, I could never understand one part of the scripture. The cloud which overspread the camp of Israel and kept off the rays of the sun by day, was a* pillar of fire by night. *It was literally so with the smoke which rose from these fires.*

The space the prairie made, and the wide sky above it, was its own wilderness and it contained its own fear. It has been said: *The children of the American Revolution hesitated forty years on the western edges of the forest because they didn't trust the grasslands.* Once you entered it, how were you to mark your place? How were you to get across it? *When I saw a settler's child tripping out of home bounds, I had a feeling that it would never get back again,* one woman on the prairie was to say. *It looked like putting out to Lake Michigan in a canoe.* The extent of its complexity was something Herman Melville understood: in *Moby-Dick*, in a chapter he calls "The Prairie," the inscrutable brow of his leviathan turned in his mind to resemble that inland sea . . . *for you see no one point precisely; not one distinct feature is revealed . . . nothing but that one broad firmament of a forehead, pleated with riddles; dumbly lowering with the doom of boats, and ships, and men . . . his great genius is declared in his doing nothing particular to prove it. It is moreover declared in his pyramidical silence . . . I but put that brow before you. Read it if you can.*

In very early ways of measuring land, length and width were attached to its agricultural value: *a perch of poor soil was longer than one of fertile soil—but in the course of the six-*

*teenth century it became standardized at 16 ½ feet. This in-
convenient length was derived from the area of agricultural
land that could be worked by one person in a day—hence
the variability. The area was reckoned to be 2 perches by
2 perches (33 feet by 33 feet). Thus a daywork amounted to
4 square perches. Conveniently, there were 40 dayworks in
an acre, the area that could be worked by a team of oxen
in a day . . .*

By the time the east was settled, the area of an acre was
standardized, but as one town sprouted another, natural advantages and obstructions often decided the limits of a farm.
Holdings were not necessarily of any uniform shape or size.
The boundaries of some Massachusetts plots laid out in the
seventeenth century fray into uncertainties: *Northward lys the
lott of Thomas Woodford beinge twelve [rods] broade and all
the marish before it to ye uplande. Next the lott of Thomas
Woodford lys the lott of Thomas Ufford beinge fourteene rod
broade and all the marish before it to ye uplande.* Boundaries
that still come down in the deeds—by the pin in the white
oak, to the stake in the ground, to the corner of a wall—con-
found surveyors to this day. The oak is likely gone, the stone
wall tumbled.

The prairie's enormity had been arrived at in an age of reason. It was mapped and marked as a grid—an idea promul-
gated by Jefferson—that took no exception to swales and
hilltops, dry spots and stony places, different soil types and
contours, which were everywhere on the prairie, however
even it appears now that it is largely gone except in the imagination. Axmen and chainmen methodically laid out the territory: *At the end of 22 yards, a tally peg was inserted, the rear
chainman came up, and the process was repeated. Ten chains*

made a furlong, 80 chains made a mile; 480 chains made one side of a township. At each mile they put in a marker post. They were instructed not to veer from the grid, no matter what they encountered, and so divided the backlands and the prairie, the world of the buffalo herds and the People of the Wind:

6   *Chains, 60 links, brook running South 20 degrees West.*

14 *Chains, 40 links, steep narrow ridge nearly 170 feet high, perpendicular. Covered on east side with many bushes and weeds . . . Golden rod, the latter when timely used, and properly applied has been found efficacious in curing the bite of the most venomous Snake. Soil on ridge equal parts of sand and black mould.*

13 *Chains, gradual descent, thicket with trees, the whole of the distance was cut through for the Chain carriers to pass.*

5   *Chains, 63 links, makes two miles.*

One forty-acre parcel might be boggy, the next might lack a ready source of water—settlers were advised to see their land before purchase, and the smart ones did. It was not the best way to create one farm and then another, divorced as it was from any assessment of the agricultural value of the land. It was not the best way to create one community and then another—the grid created no natural settlement center. But it was an idea with a heretofore unknown clarity of demarcation, which still exists: *"When you see how easy it is to use the land survey,"* declares Lance Bishop, chief of the BLM's *geographic services in California, "you have to admire Thomas Jefferson's foresight in choosing a grid. Every parcel of land has an identity. As an example, I've just bought a five acre parcel, and I can go back to the original records and see the shape of the original property, where it was first platted, where the original markers were set, and all subsequent records. It's very clear; there's no ambiguity about what you own."* Such a grid, as one commentator noted, had a purpose far beyond that of providing land for individual farmers and their families: *A uniform, invariable shape that took no account of springs or hills or swamps was an obstacle to efficient agriculture, but to a financier tracking the rise and fall in land values, it was a great convenience. The grid, designed by Thomas Jefferson to create republican farmers, also turned out to be ideal for buying, trading, and speculating.*

At the start settlement still proceeded as it had back east, little by little, along the braided rivers. The prairie might have given the settlers a deep rich sod to cultivate, and saved them the labor of felling trees to create fields, but nearness to watercourses was their only assurance of transport in a world of scarce roads, and the woodlands that ribboned the waterways provided the lumber for houses, barns, fencing, fuel for cooking fires and heat in winter. The soil they encountered, built up by countless years of grasses growing and dying, could be measured in feet rather than inches, and was thick with organic matter. It clung to the cast-iron plows that had served the eastern farmers, and had to be scraped off—a frustrating and inefficient process until John Deere invented the self-scouring steel plow. Even then, the heft of the work was enormous. A settler might not cut into the big bluestem himself but employ professional "prairie breakers" with their oversized plows. As the settlers along the rivers fought fires and plowed firebreaks and mowed fields, as the bluestem disappeared, the natural fuel sources for prairie fires disappeared. Once the fires stopped—fires that had always kept woodlands from establishing themselves on the same ground—saplings reappeared on lands that weren't plowed or used for pasture. Farmers let them grow, and the tallgrass prairie began to settle into a pattern of cultivated fields, pasture, and small woodlots.

E ven Jefferson understood that his dream had *peopled the Western States by silently breaking up those on the Atlantic.* The rumor of richer prairie sod to the west did spur the abandonment of New England farms, but additional factors contributed to the depopulation of the countryside. By the late eighteenth century not only had careless farming practices drawn down the fertility on formerly rich land, Massachusetts by then lacked enough tillable soil for agriculture to support its population: farming had overextended itself into rougher country with lower natural fertility, which produced marginal crop yields and only a meager living for its inhabitants. These poorer outlying farms would be among the first to be given up on, yet even those brief clearings retain a presence on the land to this day. Climb any of the hills on the low ranges or the scattered monadnocks of central New England rising just a few thousand feet above sea level, and after you've walked through beech forest and hemlock and lifted yourself up ledges, you just might walk into a scrubby clearing where walls mark the boundaries of old sheep meadows. The foot-path through the pasture will be trodden down to bedrock, and the soil alongside the path supports only the cold, hardy life of mosses and lichen. Sheep haven't grazed there for over a century, but the weather is harsh enough so that large trees haven't been able to reestablish themselves. Every once in a while you can detect a certain amount of care in the way the stones have been laid for a wall, and you get an idea of what had been invested in such wild country. As you look out on the vast forested hills of your own century, it's hard to believe anyone would think to farm there, or that brief, quiet efforts could have rung such a persistent change.

Those who left the farms not only went west, they went to the industrial cities that were quickly rising up along the larger rivers in the Northeast as manufacturing became an increasing necessity. Industry was a means to prevent the further exodus of the population from the eastern states, but it was also deemed essential for the further development of the country. In the wake of the War of 1812, as cheap British goods threatened to flood the American markets and undermine fledgling industries, even Thomas Jefferson capitulated to the larger necessity of manufacturing. *We must now place the manufacturer by the side of the agriculturist,* he writes in 1816. *Shall we make our own comforts, or go without them, at the will of a foreign nation? He, therefore, who is now against domestic manufacture, must be for reducing us either to dependence on that foreign nation, or to be clothed in skins, and to live like wild beasts in dens and caverns. I am not one of these; experience has taught me that manufactures are now as necessary to our independence as to our comfort . . .*

In our own lower Merrimack Valley, one of the earliest areas of the country to be industrialized, textile cities—Lowell, Manchester, Haverhill, and Lawrence—sprouted along every substantial drop in the river. Alongside those cities, some places in the valley where the soils are rich enough—or the farmers tenacious enough—have held on to agriculture; a few farms even now have been in the same family for almost four hundred years. But on other farms, the years had been discouraging enough for families to consider change, and they looked to the cities for those changes. As the cities grew, not only by pulling people away from the farms but by attracting new immigrants from abroad, they also created new markets for farmers, and some of the outlying farms, rather than being abandoned, were sold to recent immigrants from southern and eastern Europe and the Middle East.

To take on farmland where others had already come and gone, to gain your ground there, is its own kind of succession. The rain and sun and shadow that decay one world feed the other. Before my grandparents bought our farm in 1901, it saw several owners. Richardson sold to Packard, Packard sold to my grandfather, who bought not only the buildings and land but the horses and hens and chickens, the carts and feed, the hoes and harrows. I can imagine one life stood in for another in the nature of the works and days, that the plowing and planting required to keep the place going didn't change much from owner to owner.

For my grandparents, possession of a farm meant they would have greater freedom and control over their lives than the city offered, but it also meant they hadn't the ease of living among other Middle Eastern immigrants. How insular they must have felt, and how peculiar their lives must have seemed to the neighboring farmers, the eggplant and chickpeas, spiced lamb, pine nuts, dried figs, and pistachios at their table, the guttural tongue spoken among the white clapboard barns, the pastures, and orchards. My grandparents would have been compelled to speed up their efforts at assimilation: their children were never to speak more than a halting Arabic. No matter their effort to blend in, the natural suspicion of their foreignness would have been exacerbated by the knowledge that their presence underscored the fading away of a particular world, one that had been the sole province of the Yankee farmer. That suspicion is hinted at in a few veiled stories of the family past, something about a neighbor continually trying to expose my grandfather's hard cider enterprise.

I have no doubt the insularity contributed to the great sense of fidelity among them, but my father and his brothers and sisters always chose to remember to us how one world grew into the other, how they sat down with their neighbors at box parties and danced with them at the Grange Hall, how out of the blue, a Yankee neighbor was to offer a loan to one of my uncles to attend college. Sometimes I like to imagine that within this mixture of stability and instability there is a strange turning of Jefferson's dream. In his travels in Europe he had once imagined how the southern European farmers would be of advantage to the American soil: *Emigrants too from the Mediterranean would be of much more value to our country in particular . . . They bring with them a skill in agriculture and other arts better adapted to our climate. I believe that had our country been peopled thence we should now have been farther advanced in rearing the several things which our country is capable of producing.*

Just like your father and his father," people would say once my brother had grown old enough to have his own ideas about things to be done. As long as he remained young—the boy on the tractor, the kind you see all the time—a twelve- or thirteen-year-old—puffed out with the responsibility in one moment, worn with the weight of it in another, older than his peers by virtue of work—for as long as he remained that boy, I imagine there had been more dream than difficulty. As he grew into his teenage years, when my father would call to my brother repeatedly to get up for work on early summer mornings, my brother willfully slept on. Some days they'd sit beside each other at lunch and again at dinner, speaking to one another only to disagree. It may be a trick of memory but their arguments seemed to dominate the household then. The rest of us receded in their wake.

As my brother became a grown man and expressed more fully his own desires about building a modern greenhouse, and then a larger farmstand, the tensions between them grew even more pronounced. The drugs he used withered everyone's trust, so that even his modest, sensible ideas—"It's not worth keeping the orchard, it's been losing money for years," he'd often say—were greeted with averted eyes and skepticism. Sometimes when he entered a room he'd walk into silence.

Whatever the situation of the land, there is always the lay of the family as well, which has as much to do with the success of farming as anything else. Farm life intensifies the demands on a family—I know it did in ours. Living with those arguments had to color my concept of the farm, and I don't wonder that in the conversations among farmers I overheard at trade shows and yearly meetings, amid the talk of sales and row covers, I seemed always to pick up on an undercurrent of conflict. When I heard an old farmer ponder whether it was time to give the farm over to a son who by then was in his sixties, I could recognize something darkly humorous about it—I retell it, and it always raises a chuckle—but I also felt sorrow. I could sense the long years of forbearance within the family.

Though I haven't been to a trade show in a long time, old voices still swirl in my head as if I'd heard them just yesterday: "He was the oldest, he drank the wine, tasted the food, then they all ate. He's got Parkinson's—advanced. He'd just go out into the field and stand there until it got too bad, and then not at all. The kid comes back and wants to do it the new way. He just wanted to be consulted." "The boys will never keep the place together. You'll never have the nicer things in life by farming and there's always one who wants more." "I worked beside him for forty years, I changed the diapers on him, and then he just leases it out without even talking to me."

Upon my return to the farm, having witnessed for years those disagreements only from a distance, I suppose I thought that my helping out could alleviate some of the tensions that had made our world feel insular and fragile. I didn't fully comprehend how intertwined the relationship between my father and brother truly was.

"I don't know what to do," my father said to me one day in a moment when he was bewildered by my brother's intransigence.

"Maybe he should go his own way," I inched, thinking how it would release them both, release everyone.

"Cruel, aren't you?" he said quietly, and I half believed him. I could see then that there was no changing the direction of things, and perhaps that understanding was part, though never all, of the reason I would only allow myself to invest so much in that summer work. Even if I had wanted the farm to be my life, I knew that no matter how much I worked, a future—a real future—was unimaginable. It is a strange thing now to realize however much their relationship kept the rest of us at bay, it is likely also true that had my brother not stayed on my father could not have run the farm as a business into his eighties, and it would not exist at all.

I'd been back working for a few growing seasons when I saw the Midwest for the first time. I'd decided as the year wound down to its stillness in the spare world after the frost, and my exhaustion gradually lifted, that I'd take advantage of the winter to get away. During those first years back, in addition to being confounded by the stressful relationship between my father and brother, I was more self-conscious about my return than I am now—as if I was going against the grain—and I was haunted by the thought that I might be cutting off possibilities or making myself smaller, so to strike out for friends in Montana and then Utah on a crisp January dawn seemed freeing. I remember how much I anticipated the trip, was buoyed by the idea of the West, of the far distances between my friends, even as I worried about the snows I might encounter on my way there. "They won't let you through the passes without chains," friends would say to me. "Make sure you have blankets in the car in case you break down." "You always need to be watching the weather."

I imagined the Midwest as something to simply get through quickly as I slipped south onto I-70 in hopes of avoiding the worst of the snows for travel. As the pines gave way to deciduous patches here and there and the open spaces increased, I began to see more and more farms, large ones, enormous. The original forty-acre holdings that had fed a family and a few others had, over time, become farms that fed thirty others, then fifty, a hundred, one hundred and twenty-nine at last count. For the first time I began to understand ourselves in relation to something larger. Even in their dormancy I could sense the extent of the dream—the size of one field could be larger than our entire place—but what struck me even more was a feeling that there was no room for intimacy in that landscape. The day would glitter on over wide, wintry expanses where the attempts at intimacy were stark and obvious: the farmhouses were obscured behind tall conifers planted as windbreaks. Everything existed in relation to the horizontal. Nothing radiated out from a town—the innate loneliness of the configuration of the grid.

Still, I could sense a community of farming in that world. Every day I would start out in the dark, drive a few hours, then pull off the highway for breakfast. Inevitably I walked into a world of farms. Amid the aroma of coffee and bacon frying, the clattering dishes and steamed-up plate glass, men in peaked caps and overalls sat on stools and in booths, along with grain salesmen and Agway reps, and talked to each other about farming, farming, farming. The crops may have been different from ours, and the scale much larger, but the kind of talk felt assuring and familiar, and made that world seem whole: "The price of soybeans . . ." "The new cultivator does the work in half the time . . ." I'd drive on for another several hundred miles and find them at lunch, one day and the next.

On the winter morning I began to drive through Kansas I'd started out in the dark as usual, expecting nothing more than a long day across a flat state and meals among farmers. But as the dawn lightened the sky I could sense how the land was rising up on either side of me, and I found myself growing attentive to some shouldering presence. In a little while I saw rime everywhere on hills of dried, stunted winter bluestem. There was no height to hold me—the grass had gone to its reserves—but the swell and the space held me, and the color of the grasses, which was as tawny as the summer pelt of a fawn. I'd come upon a vestige of the tallgrass prairie— and a vestige is all that remains of it, along railbeds, in old cemeteries, on substantial hills. Later on I was to understand that I had arrived in the Flint Hills, which had always been too steep to plow and, with their shallow, rocky soils, had been too poor to cultivate. Cattle may have replaced buffalo there as the tallgrass prairie became tallgrass pasture, but the dream of the grid meant little to it, and while elsewhere the grasses were plowed under, and the soil was planted in row crops, and the prairie became known as the corn belt, the big bluestem on those hills continued to weave its mat of roots. Now the Flint Hills stand as the last large expanse of tallgrass prairie, and are preserved as a presettlement ecosystem where research scientists measure biotic production, trace the fate of the soils, and examine the effects of fire and grazing on the vegetation. Sometimes they burn grasses methodically in an attempt to replicate and understand the old nature of the land.

As the day came on and the prairie hills rose to their true immensity, I found myself under a sky that was even wider than the Nantucket sky I'd known years ago, wider than the salt marsh sky. I was on the highway going sixty, sixty-five, pulled forward by my aim but watching sideward. Maybe I was susceptible to it—something so immense and full of forgetting—because I'd been traveling through all that sequestered farmland in the days before. Even as Kansas settled into cultivation again, the prairie wouldn't leave me, and now my memory of those hills has grown outsized, living on in my mind more than the Colorado Rockies and the red rock canyons of Utah I was to see afterward. I'm sure the Flint Hills are the one place I would recognize again, and not only for their sheer singularity—the last wild is not a sea anymore, only an island; I think more and more of what I imagine to be their resilience and patience. I have dreamt of walking into those grasses, of the feeling I would have of open wildness, of my own smallness among something so endless, a world clear to the horizon with no goal other than to be its stark, intricate, immeasurable self.

I have never been able to think of anything so large as the brow of a whale or the doom of ships when I've looked out on our land. But if, within the summer stillness, you stand in the right place among the worn hills and the leafed-out hampered branches of our orchard trees, the earth can seem to hold as much coiled energy as a cresting wave or a van Gogh landscape. And sometimes within the confines of an old meadow full of short grasses and rocky outcrops, I have imagined the emerging granites to be the backs of small mammals breaching the swells of a watery surface. Our houses are small craft upon it, but there's no place for the *Pequod* running under full sail, or the *Rachel* appearing on the horizon of a miraculous abeyance: *The unharming sharks, they glided by as if with padlocks on their mouths; the savage sea-hawks sailed with sheathed beaks . . .*

3

THE NEW CITY

It could change—the way memory is always at risk of changing, being one insight away from a recollecting of the self—but I feel a resolution when I remember my father. An ease had grown between us, one we never would have had were it not for having worked together in his late years. That ease stemmed in part from mutually dependent work but also from a lightness of expectations. We had no history: our dealings were simpler and freer than the long-standing ones my father had with my brother, caught up as they were with the expectations of inheritance, from which I'd always been separate.

When I worked on the farm as a child my chores were partial, ones I shared with my sister, my girl cousins, the neighbor who'd crashed his motorcycle at the bend in the road and had a plate in his head: picking strawberries, picking beans, three- or four-hour stints selling corn and tomatoes. The farm was at the heart of all the talk during summer lunches then. My father and Pete, his right-hand man—and later, my brothers—

filled the air with discussions about what needed to be done: "You might as well plow down the Salem Road piece." "The rye will be coming tomorrow." "The Macs are reddening up pretty nice." "I should put some water on the corn." I couldn't place my voice within the conversation, and my mother's voice was absent, too.

After I returned, as I ran the farm store and saw to the wholesale orders and kept accounts—work I came to enjoy for its straightforwardness—I thought of the time as an interim. I carried with me the notion that my future ran underground all through the long summers, that it resided in the wintertime when I'd return to writing again. Even so, I took to the work wholeheartedly, and when I'd sometimes join my parents for lunch on a summer day, my father and I would naturally talk about what had to be done: "We'll need more lettuce and radishes by morning." "The corn sales are starting to quiet down." "The Huntleys want some tomatoes. I could drive them over tomorrow afternoon if there's a free truck." Necessity made a world of its own, running on at its certain pace. There was always so much to do, and time, time, time, you were always working against time, and the heat, and the rain. Each day was one hurry after another, and I always felt I didn't have a moment to think about anything else. My mother would be as quiet as she'd always been, setting down a platter of ham, dishes of steaming corn or baked tomatoes, olives, cheese, bread. One day I was helping to clear the dishes—I'm sure I was abstracted, already thinking ahead to the work of the afternoon—and as I set them in the sink and began to head on my way, she turned to me and said: "It's always about the farm, isn't it?"

It was, and I have never thought of my mother as having

any attachment to the work of it. She'd been raised in the city of Lawrence, six miles to the east, and had lived on the third floor of a tenement until she married my father in the early 1950s. The world he made for her was almost as distinct from the farm as that of a suburban housewife. The Cape Cod colonial he had built is down the road from the original farmhouse and is distinguished from the fields and orchards by a trimmed lawn in front and back. There are no barns, outbuildings, or add-ons anywhere near it. Every once in a while there'd be a tractor parked in the drive when my father or brother had left off plowing and come right in to lunch, but no one passing would think a farmer lived there. Some farmwives up and down the road helped with haying and planting—it wasn't unusual—but my father had never asked my mother to be part of that world, and I think it was a mark of pride with him that he could keep her apart from it. He brought the farm to the door. Eggplant, tight and gleaming, sat in baskets on the porch. Squash, tomatoes, peppers. Late in August he left her corn by the bushel, which she would freeze for the winter. In September, butternut squash, Macs for applesauce, Cortlands for pies, and after Cortlands, Northern Spies.

Even the old farmhouse, I can see, had separated itself from the working farm by then. When my aunts and uncles were growing up, work moved easily in and out of the house, everyone was involved. As at every farm along the road, men and boys chopped wood and hitched up the teams just beyond the kitchen doorway. Women cut seed potatoes on the stoop, or plucked chickens. Children milked cows, fed chickens, gathered eggs, hauled water from the well. Bertha and Del, the oldest, also saw to their brothers. I've heard it said of Bertha more than once: "She was like a mother to them . . ."

The summer kitchen of the farmhouse eventually was turned into a sitting room. The barn, silo, and windmill: gone. These days a tractor or two will be stored in the carriage house, but mostly it's a place filled with disused tools—scythes, rusted collars, broken hoes, ropes. The chain of buildings attached to the house is like a vestigial limb, a phantom of old use. Part of the separation of house from farmland was inevitable, a consequence of modernization. As wood fuel was replaced by oil, and kerosene by electricity, as salt and ice gave way to refrigeration, the farm became more integrated with the world at large, and more dependent on it for its energy and food. The household required less of the immediate world.

When the farm became my father's to work, as his brothers moved on to their own lives and occupations, as chickens and cows were sold, the division between house and land became even more distinct. My Uncle Joe continued to tinker in the shed and to keep his own garden plot to the side—there's still some straggling asparagus and rhubarb that sprout up spring after spring—and Bertha continued to walk through the fields and woods, but the farm was fully a business in their later years, and had grown into a definition beyond them. The work of it was done by men and boys outside the family, while the farmhouse remained the repository of family life and memory. Late in their lives Bertha, Del, and Joe sat on the porch in their green rocking chairs and watched three seasons pass. Their yard was swept neat, and the irises along the old hitching post bloomed and faded in late spring. The farm they knew continued in their imagination: "Pop would tell me to go get a chicken that had stopped laying. 'Are you sure?' he'd ask. 'I'm sure,' I said. Boy, did I catch hell when he pulled out that string of eggs . . ." "I used to carry the milk over to the well. Imagine that—trusting me with the milk—I was nine years old!"

There is a small oil painting I love, *Florentine Villas* by Paul Klee. On first seeing it from a distance, I could only make out muted blurry patches of color, reds and earth tones that appeared sun-bleached and washed so you'd think they had been stitched together out of old cloth. As you peer closer you see that the patches are washes of paint patterned by Klee's spidery, scratchy marks, so simply delicate and certain they seem to hark back to the drawings on the caves at Lascaux. There are no people in the picture, but the human imprint is patterned everywhere on those washed squares. Some of the patches represent homes, others mark row crops, vines, stairwells, roads. Only in looking more closely can you distinguish the cultivated from the built. The vines and crops are softer human marks than the stairs, walls, and roads, but there isn't much distinction in the order between outdoors and in. The wild with its different idea is somewhere beyond. Where is it we live? I remember thinking as I looked at the households and the care spreading out from them, and how integral they seemed, each to each.

While many of the things of the old work life still hang in the carriage house—moldering husks disintegrating into themselves—after Bertha died we carefully went through the household, all of us, and settled out things and carried them away to our own houses for remembrance: hats and coats, letters, books, lamps, plates, sifters, china pitchers, mixing bowls. It took so much time. We'd unearth one thing and then another, and each had memories and stories attached to it. What I remember most clearly, though, is the late February evening half a year after Bertha's death when all of us nieces met to divide our aunts' jewelry. More than seventy pieces had been found in the boxes in the upper drawers of the dressers, in the safe set in the old fireplace, in all the lightless sequester of the house. "Christ, where did it all come from?" someone said. Time had worn away a little of the luster of the metals, a little of the shine of the stones. The cardboard boxes were brown, and the plump velvet cushions within the velvet boxes were threadbare.

After a dinner of fish stew and a salad of baby greens we cleared the table and sat down again to draw our lots out of a ceramic bowl. One of my cousins had assigned a number to all seventy pieces, the gold bracelet and gold cross, the diamond rings as well as the imitation pearls and the plastic necklaces. Which was Bertha's, which Del's, we didn't always know. None of us remembered them having worn much more than a brooch on a lamb's-wool sweater, or a necklace and matching earrings to a formal gathering. A few of the pieces were fine things cherished and deliberately handed down from their own mother: a wedding ring, a watch, and several hammered-gold bracelets. Most had been gifts from their brothers, given at Christmas and birthdays, or as souvenirs from trips. There were cameos from Italy, one who loved the sea gave scrimshaw, the one who went to Hawaii brought back shell beads.

We talked on about the trips we'd taken—"Provence! You're so lucky"—and Boston restaurants, careers, children. "We can open the floor to trades afterward," one of my cousins sang out, and we joked about a gaudy coral piece: "You could get away with it on a black coat." We said we'd fix the watches, adjust the rings, and polish up some of the metals. "Oh, you got a good one," my cousin in charge said as she set down a gold cross in front of me. "Oh yes," another affirmed. I stared down at it, not knowing what to do, or how to feel. It was one of the oldest pieces, which everyone had seen in an old photograph hanging around a teenage Del's neck on a fine chain that brought it to rest in the center of her breast. She was wearing a bowed and flounced white dress and had one firm arm around a shy, inward Bertha—dressed the same—and another around two of her baby brothers, as protective and determined as I'd ever seen her. I couldn't imagine ever wearing the cross, not so anyone could see it anyway, not with the force of its convictions. "And a not so good one," my cousin continued as she set down a choker made of false blue pearls. Everyone laughed and I let myself be drawn back into the laughter. We held the pins up to our jerseys and lifted the earrings to the sides of our faces until all the numbers had been drawn and all pieces distributed, and we each had before us a little glittering mound built of paste and pearls and gold and plate.

I think I can trace a faint line, scratchy yet certain as Klee's, that separates farmhouses from farmland. It extends back at least to the nineteenth century, when New England girls followed the roads down from rocky, marginal Vermont and New Hampshire farms to meet industry in the first textile cities along the rivers. These young women were the first to lose their place within the farm families. During the first centuries of settlement they'd been a steady part of the household economy, bringing in added income as they'd spun and woven wool and flax into cloth for the family not only to wear but to sell for additional income. They'd also made cheese, butter, and brooms, tended the family garden, helped their mothers with the demands of cooking and cleaning, raising children, caring for the sick. With the advent of the textile mills, even rural families found it was cheaper to buy cloth than to rely on homespun, and in the stores their farm-made goods could no longer compete. The textile mills offered a small income to the girls, and work there meant one less mouth to feed at home. The mill wasn't to provide a constant place for them, and most never envisioned it as their entire future: they worked to build up a dowry, or while awaiting marriage. Some worked through the winter and returned to the farm in summer.

Their early letters home bespeak a readiness for experience, a determination and acceptance, often an appealing openness. *I get along very well with my work. I can doff as fast as any girl in our room,* one young woman wrote home. *I think I shall have frames before long. The usual time allowed for learning is six months but I think I shall have frames before I have been in three as I get along so fast. I think that the factory is the best place for me . . .* And in a subsequent letter: *You wanted to know what I am doing. I am at work in a spinning room and tending four sides of a warp which is one girls work. The overseer tells me that he never had a girl get along better than I do and that he will do the best he can by me. I stand it well, though they tell me I am growing very poor. I was paid nine shillings a week last payment and am to have more this one though we have been out considerable for backwater which will take off a good deal* . . .

They might see the city in a way that was not imagined in the larger discourses, with a softer division in the world: *I arrived here safe and sound, after being well jolted over the rocks and hills of New Hampshire; and when (it was then evening) a gentleman in the stage first pointed out Lowell to me, with its lights twinkling through the gloom, I could think of nothing but Passampscot swamp when brilliantly illuminated by "lightning bugs." You, I know, will excuse all my "up-country" phrases, for I have not yet got the rust off* . . . *You will ask what I have already seen* . . . *There are stores filled with beautiful goods upon either side, and some handsome public buildings* . . . *I waited, one day, to see the cars come in from Boston. They moved, as you know, very swiftly but not so much like "a streak of lightning" as I had anticipated. If all country girls are like me their first impressions of a city are far below their previous conceptions, and they think there is more difference than there really is. Little as I know of it now I see that the difference is more apparent than real. There are the same passions at work beneath another surface.*

But as the textile industry matured, the speed of the machines increased, production lines grew more frantic, and working conditions worsened. The young woman who'd believed the factory was the best place for her reported a far more sobering story just three years later: *It is very hard indeed and sometimes I think I shall not be able to endure it. I never worked so hard in my life but perhaps I shall get used to it. I shall try hard to do so for there is no other work that I can do unless I spin and that I shall not undertake on any account. I presume you have heard before this that the wages are to be reduced on the 20th of this month . . . The compa-nies pretend they are losing immense sums every* day *and therefore they are obliged to lessen the wages, but this seems perfectly absurd to me for they are constantly making* repairs *and it seems to me that this would not be if there were really any danger of their being obliged to* stop *the mills.*

Eventually most of the young women were to lose their place again as worsening conditions in the factory made the work untenable for them and immigrant laborers took over, but the experience had changed their options. However much more softly they'd seen the divisions in the world, however great their fidelity to home and family, when they married many chose not to marry farmers. Perhaps they'd become accustomed to the busier, more varied world of the city and didn't wish to return to the remote life of their childhoods. But they also knew the demands that world would bring with it: *They contemn the calling of their father,* one nineteenth-century critic wrote, *and will nine times out of ten, marry a mechanic in preference to a farmer. They know that marrying a farmer is a serious business. They remember their worn-out mothers.*

With the coming of industry the physical change in the countryside was rapid and extreme. Thoreau was witness to one such transformation: *At the time of our voyage Manchester was a village of about two thousand inhabitants, where we landed for a moment to get some cool water, and where an inhabitant told us that he was accustomed to go across the river into Goffstown for his water. But now, after*

*nine years, as I have been told and indeed have witnessed, it
contains sixteen thousand inhabitants. From a hill on the road
between Goffstown and Hooksett, four miles distant, I have
since seen a thunder shower pass over, and the sun break out
and shine on a city there, where I had landed nine years before in the fields to get a draught of water; and there was wav-
ing the flag of its museum,—where "the only perfect skeleton
of a Greenland or river whale in the United States" was to be
seen . . .*

Where my mother's native city of Lawrence now stands,
there had been scarcely a house on the land in the early eighteenth century, until the skirmishes with the Indian tribes died
away and some of the settlers moved from the villages on the
outlying hard rock hills to homesteads nearer their plantings.
A crossroads settlement was the nearest thing to a village on
that plain; there was even less then to mark any kind of cen-
trality than there had been when the Agawam gathered near
the drop in the river, which would come to be known as Bodwell's Falls, to fish for shad and salmon. There'd been
alewives in the tributaries. The floodplain soil was suitable for
corn and beans.

The river's course there was so wide it had been considered
an obstacle in the colonial world. Not only was it difficult to
cross—in places near Lawrence it was over seven hundred feet
wide—it was impossible to make use of, unlike the smaller
rivers and streams where a few men could construct a dam for
modest power with wooden cribs or branches and stumps. By
the early nineteenth century there were still fewer than several
hundred settlers in the area, which was kept largely in cornfields, rye fields, orchards, woodlands. The place was sometimes known as Moose Country. History wasn't much more

than anecdote, little legends. In exchange for a roll of cloth, it's said, a settler purchased of the Indians the rights for all the lands he could surround in a day's travel through the forest. And there remain some things the explanation of which is lost, if ever there was one. When the town on the south side of the river came to be known as the Plain of Sodom, the town to the north called itself Gomorrah in return.

During the emerging years of the industrial revolution, Bodwell's Falls was still seen as a quandary: the river was so wide that if a dam were to be built, it would have to be the largest in the Western world. So, while other places on the river—narrower expanses with greater drops—were dammed, as industry followed the old patterns of settlement north, as the machines sped up and output increased, the world around Bodwell's Falls remained agricultural.

The dam that was eventually designed for the city of Lawrence there represented the long accumulation of architect Charles Storrow's education in Europe and America. At the time of its building in the three years between 1845 and 1848, such a span still had never been successfully crossed by a dam. For the project Storrow studied the structure and defects of timber dams—their tendency to rot, and their inability to withstand severe overtopping. He inspected dams on the Croton River, the Schuylkill, the Kennebec, and studied the designs of English dams. He pored over treatises on retaining walls and mapped equations concerning the effects of the force of water on stone. He found no strong examples to draw on, though his studies helped him to eliminate timber and earthen dams from consideration, and also helped him to structure the masonry dam he eventually designed. The project was so large and expensive he knew he had to get it right on the first try, since it would be impossible to repair. Any broach would spell disaster—financial and otherwise—for the city. It would not only destroy the mills in Lawrence but wreak havoc on the cities downstream.

Storrow designed the city as well, he laid out its streets, factories, and houses. It was built in concert with the dam and seemed to rise up almost overnight. A nineteenth-century eye saw it this way: *For two centuries the river and the land literally ran to waste; but sparsely settled, in productiveness meagrely requiting the tiller's industry, it seemed destined . . . to a career of barrenness and comparative worthlessness, until the splendid water-power caught the eye of the sagacious manufacturer, when a change, rapid as wonderful, came over the scene: the desert waste grew green, active, busy life dispelled the unpleasant silence, and the solitary place forthwith resounded with the cheerful rattle of machinery, the ring of the anvil, the vigorous strokes of the artisan and mechanic, the whirl and bustle of trade, and the constant rush of steadily augmenting throngs where once the few hardy fishermen, along the falls, at the mouth of the Shawsheen and Spicket, captured the magnificent and delicious salmon, the bony shad, and the slimy, squirming eel, a change is wrought sudden and complete.*

The effort was exhaustive: *In all the region in which the city now stands there was no spot where one could escape the din and dust . . . Beginning at the gneiss ledge, situated nearly two miles south, the stone from which composes the river wall and mill foundations—or at North Andover, three miles east, then the depository of bricks and lumber by railway—or at Pelham, some eight miles west, from whence came the granite for the dam—there was an almost endless string of slow plodding teams, loaded to the utmost, all centering from the dam to the Spicket River to deposit their loads. But here were not the only signs of activity. All over the place buildings were rising with most astonishing celerity. For twelve hours a day, the heavy teams, here removing hills, there filling valleys, or loaded with building materials, plodded through the suffocating dust of dry weather, or the almost bottomless mud of the rainy season . . . In 1846 and early 1847 there was a large accession to the population. Mechanics, merchants, physicians and lawyers began to locate here, and order began to rise out of chaos. In 1846 the first religious service was held, and by the following year most of the leading sects were established here. In October 1846, the first newspaper was issued . . .*

The factories built there were larger than any previously constructed, production faster. Bodwell's Falls turned out to be the perfect place to meet the future, as it made possible a city more compact and efficient than any other: *The site had advantages not even enjoyed by Lowell. The banks of the river were high enough to accommodate mill islands parallel to the direction of the Merrimack, making short straight power canals and short tailraces possible. These canals could waste their excess water into small streams which flowed into the Merrimack on either side of the river . . . Where the designers of Lowell found it necessary to build over 8 miles of canals to obtain 10,000 horsepower, at Bodwell's Falls a single canal 1 mile in length delivered approximately the same power.*

The city, known first as the New City, was a mere seven square miles and almost evenly laid out on both sides of the river. Even today, when you look at a map of northeastern

Massachusetts you can see how its small round shape sets it apart, how it seems to be a concentrated drop applied atop the broad, irregular towns soldiering up and down the river.

We take the nineteenth-century cities of New England to be brick cities. Their resolute stacks and factory walls of red clay are what we see before us, and what artists render when they want to evoke those places. But the scale of those textile cities would not have been possible had men not discovered an efficient way to quarry large blocks of granite, which builders relied on for the infrastructure of the cities. Charles Storrow drew on quarries in Pelham, New Hampshire, and Cohasset, Quincy, and Rockport, Massachusetts, for the stone to build his dam. He used granite for the canal walls and the foundations of factories, and the lintels on rowhouse windows. The nineteenth century seemed to depend on granite as much as early farmers had depended on salt marsh hay, and a good measure of New England granite came from coastal quarries, from the headlands where the sand shore and salt marshes stand in abeyance.

In the colonial years those headlands remained untouched, primal, like something out of Noah's flood—*far and near we have an image of the pristine earth, the planet in its nakedness*—while colonists used so much fieldstone for cellar walls, well holes, icehouses, and fences that they began to fear they'd run out. The town of Braintree, Massachusetts, in 1715 decreed that *no person shall dig or carry off any stone on the said commons, or undivided lands upon any account whatever without license . . .* What farmer wouldn't laugh

mildly at that now, since granite has continued to surface with
every frost and thaw, with every turn of the plow and spade,
and the rough and rounded stones seem not only endless but
integral to the idea old New Englanders have of their stubborn, resistant selves. *I see him there*, wrote Frost of his wall
mender:

> *Bringing a stone grasped firmly by the top*
> *In each hand, like an old-stone savage armed.*
> *He moves in darkness as it seems to me,*
> *Not of woods only and the shade of trees . . .*

Yet even in the eighteenth century, men dreamed of the
hidden opportunity beneath soil and fieldstone. *As it is from
the surface of the ground, which we till, that we have gathered the wealth we possess, the surface of that ground is
therefore the only thing that has hitherto been known,* wrote
J. Hector St. John de Crèvecœur. *It will require the industry of
subsequent ages, the energy of future generations, ere mankind
here will have leisure and abilities to penetrate deep, and, in
the bowels of this continent, search for the subterranean
riches it no doubt contains.*

It's not that the rock could not be split. Granite, though
extremely hard, is full of stress, and will give along seams, and
crack into stratified beds: you can see that easily along Cape
Ann on the north shore of Massachusetts where the sea has
worn the rock so smooth it almost flows, and the seams have
eroded into something like the loose folds of a mammal's skin.
The job is to find the strains and apply the right touch. Ancient Egyptians jammed wood into natural cracks in granite,
wet it, and let it expand. In higher latitudes the Finns poured

water into fissures and waited for it to freeze. Others burned brushfires on the surface of the stone, and when the heat began to crack it they'd clear the ashes off and strike the weakened place with an iron ball. But such methods were inefficient and rarely yielded even-sized building blocks.

What finally made large-scale quarrying viable was a precise and patient method of splitting stone called hammering, which was first practiced at the beginning of the nineteenth century by German immigrants in the Cape Ann quarries. One man would hold the chisel while two others took turns striking it; a turn of the chisel, and they'd strike again, and again strike and turn, and stop a moment to spoon out the stone dust, then strike and turn again. In this way they tapped straight rows of holes six inches apart, about four inches deep into the stone. They then set shims and wedges, sometimes called feathers and pins, into the holes, and a man would tap into hole after hole along the line. I saw a demonstration once, lifted out of the din of a quarry. The stonecutter seemed to be playing an instrument, hammering one and then another of the wedges up and down the row and back again. Tap, tap, tapping. Then he'd pause a bit and cock his ear to the stone. "You have to listen to your stone," he said. "Let the stone breathe." His solitary effort chimed with the sound of a collateral world, the one that has always existed—particular, domestic, devoted, intent on underpinnings and doorsteps and graves. Tap, tap, tapping. Then the granite cracked quietly, no louder than mild surf falling back over cobbles.

I imagine quarried stone to be its own substance entirely, wrought out of the rising dust of the pits—deep, deeper, deepest—amid a cacophony, granite not just for home truths but perfect for the ambitions of the nineteenth century: hewn and hammered, worked straight and smooth toward an endless desire for dams, columns, bridges, banks, post offices, and dry docks, the eagles of the Boston Customs House, a monument to Myles Standish, paving blocks for the streets of Boston and the streets of Havana. *Quarry*, from the Middle French *quarre*, meaning cut stone, from the Latin *quadrum*, square. And it did make square a world that had once satisfied itself with cobbles and fieldstone. Cape Ann granite turned out to be the strongest in New England, the same as that which had been hauled out of the quarries of Aswan: mottled green and mottled gray, glinting with quartz, the sapstone turning a pinkish red in time. When it was finished and polished it gleamed the way fieldstone never had, and it seems Emerson was right: every new relation *is* a new word.

Granite, *grano*, *granum*, grainy old photos of the Finns and Swedes and Italians at their workstations. They have the intent eyes of birds, and barrel chests. Behind them stretch canyons of stone where everything is happening at once: men preparing to blast rock, men dwarfed by the derricks they are operating and the dimension stone being hauled up out of the pits. Dust is rising and settling on the shoulders and caps and in the lungs of quarry workers bent to the center of the noise. Scattered around the rims of the pits are wooden sheds and rigged canvas shelters where cutters are shaping blocks or carving decorative pieces and monuments. *You can look through those shed windows when the sun is shining and that old dust is everywhere . . . It used to get so dusty in there you couldn't see the other men.*

Out beyond, between the larger quarries that produced dimension stone, were scattered small one- or two-man quarries where men hammered out paving blocks. Their hands may have been burned, broken, and callused; still, it's said, they could sense in their fingertips where the rock would give most easily. They'd cut and chip one hundred and fifty to two hundred blocks a day, at five cents a block, thirty-two different sizes of pavers before they were through: Manhattan Specials, Washingtons, Philadelphia blocks, Belgian blocks, Cuba blocks, crosswalk stones. *You have to take advantage of your stone . . . You can't be afraid of the stone. If you are, you won't hit it hard enough to get anywhere, but if you hit it too hard, you'll spoil it.*

When the quarries were in full production, pumps ran day and night to keep the flooding at bay as the men worked down and down to get out the stone. The deeper they cut, the fewer seams they encountered in the rock, and the larger the blocks they could haul out, so they might have felt that if they cut deep enough they'd encounter a fractureless absolute. Maybe that's what they were working toward at the height of the quarrying days, when millions of tons of stone were blasted from the headlands, shaped, and shipped—they sold everything but the sound, it was said, even the stone chips and the dust, which gardeners spread around the roots of their fruit trees. *People couldn't imagine life any other way . . .*

By the time my mother's parents arrived in Lawrence the city had been increasing in density for more than fifty years. The place was never to grow beyond its seven square miles, but as its industrial ambitions continued to increase during the nineteenth century its influence reached even into the North Country. To regulate the level of the river so as to prevent shutdowns and idleness especially in summer, the Essex Company, members of which had founded both Lawrence and Lowell, gained control of water near the source of the Merrimack River, at Newfound Lake, Squam, and Winnipesaukee. They built dams to control the flow. In the low-water season, as they raised the river they flooded the hayfields of farmers a hundred miles north of the city.

Within the city, as the size of the factories and the speed of the machines increased, the labor strife increased, with brief walkouts during the late nineteenth and early twentieth centuries, and major strikes in 1882 and 1912. The scale of the tragedies increased as well. It had been a mark of pride that only one man had lost his life during construction of what was to become known as the Great Stone Dam. The early mill deaths had occurred in ones and twos as in the first years at Lowell, when a young girl would write to her father: *My life and health are spared while others are cut off. Last Thursday one girl fell down and broke her neck which caused instant death . . . The same day a man was killed by the cars. Another had nearly all of his ribs broken. Another was nearly killed by falling down and having a bale of cotton fall on him.* When the poorly cast iron pillars of the Pemberton Mill in Lawrence gave way on January 10, 1860, the building collapsed onto 670 workers. A few hours later, a lantern carried by a rescue worker broke, and the ensuing fire raged out of control. Eighty-eight people died, 275 were injured. The majority of those killed were women, many from overseas. The majority in the mills at that time were still women.

The tenements low on the plain grew more crowded as new tenements were built on back lots. In 1911 it was reckoned that one-third of the population lived on one-thirteenth of the city's land: over 33,000 persons on 300 acres. *It is not a home but a tool-box,* a critic of the city's tenements wrote. But women would make what they could of the life. They watched their neighbors' children and shared cooking utensils which they hung on the outsides of the houses. *I used to hear my mother call me from the kitchen and the smell of food told me it was time to eat,* one remembered. *But when I'd get there sometimes, it wasn't my mother, but a voice from next door, through the window! I could reach out and eat off my neighbor's table we were so close . . .* And another: *You know how we workers lived then, like slaves, but we all helped each other out, that's just the way it was back then, you did for others.*

The first house my mother remembers was on the outskirts of the city, but my grandmother insisted they move to the city's center, where she could walk everywhere. Maybe she felt more at home shouldered in by her own language. She never knew more than a little broken English even into her old age, after she'd been in this country more than seventy years. She kept largely to her house and her Italian neighborhood while my grandfather became conversant in English, even took night classes while he worked in the Wood Mill. She raised my mother and her sisters to understand Italian but to speak only English in a neighborhood which was no less a village, really, than the one she'd left behind in Italy. She never learned to drive, the iceman came to the door, the milkman left bottles at the bottom of the stairs, she bought her bread, cheese, meat, fruit, and salt cod from the corner stores.

Of prospect she would have had very little: wooden tenements near crowded out a view of wooden tenements distant, and if she could have seen beyond her Italian neighborhood she would have seen the plain thick with Syrian and Belgian and French-Canadian neighborhoods. There was no way to prevent a satiety of it, to have it successively offered and in different proportions, no advantage of shifting scenes as you advanced on your way, not until the land began to rise from the plain to the west and north, and on those heights the mill owners' Victorians, with their turrets, fish-scale shingles, and finials, would keep their graceful distinctive air well into the twentieth century.

To the east and south, on the same plain as the tenements, factories lined the canals. The Wood Mill, built in 1906, was set on a sandy spot where the Agawam had once had a factory for projectile points. At the time of its construction it was the largest worsted mill in the world. Nine hundred men spent eight months building its two wings, which were each a half mile long. You'd think they'd have had to create their own word to measure it, but the way we comprehend it is to say: its four stories contained thirty acres of floor space. *Acre*: that measurement once dependent on the speed of oxen. In the thirty acres of the Wood Mill men and women processed as much as a million pounds of wool in a week. Work was measured by so much output per hour. The Poles were in the spinning rooms, the Greeks in the dyehouse, the English in the sorting room, the Italians in the weaving room. Each room contained its separate duty, dependent on another. If work in one room stopped, work in the other rooms stopped. Some workers were known for strength, others skill, everyone endurance. The acres were stacked upon acres, the machines were parceled out in rows and in columns, the workers were

spaced like apple trees: so many feet apart, so many to the
row, so many rows to the orchard.

How, out of the din of the city, would my mother have
had the opportunity to marry a farmer? She had been
working as a secretary at the New England Milk Producers
Association during the years my father served on its board.
"It's such a funny thing," she remembers, "my mother bought
a television. We must have been the first in the neighborhood
with a television. Your father would come visit on Saturday
nights, and we would watch the shows." I imagine that to my
grandparents, to have a son-in-law with a farm was an opportunity to return to some of the light and air of the village
they'd known in Italy. Those fig trees my father tried to grow
were for them. When my grandmother would come out from
Lawrence to stay with us at the farm for two weeks in early
summer, she would sit on our porch and shell peas. The husks
fell light as chaff into a basket, the peas rolled in the milk-
glass bowl, the summer was not yet fraught. She'd doze and
rouse herself, her mind would roam, she'd mutter something
in Italian and then look out on the fields of young corn, a
fresh summer breeze coming in—it was not yet the stillest of
afternoons, though the trees had arrived at their deepest
green. A long sigh: *beezina*. Runs of unintelligible Italian.
Sometimes a pidgin of Italian and English.

But for my mother, to have moved six miles east to the
farm in the 1950s—it took fifteen minutes to drive between
the two places—was to move to an utterly unfamiliar world.
I'm not sure it was any less dramatic than the journey experi-

enced by those young women coming down from the hill farms to work in the factories, entering a world that hadn't existed before, with its different understanding of work and time, which they let change them. Emerson said they were born with knives in their brains. My mother will laugh today at the memory of the woman she'd been back then, buying corn for my father at the grocery store. "I thought I'd surprise him . . ." I can't begin to imagine what he himself thought, with the first block of the thirty acres of it just ripening outside the door, as she set the ears down on their lone dinner table.

When she tells that story I know she is stunned by time: it seems to her it happened yesterday. Yet she has long since grown into the world around her. She may never have participated in the farmwork, but the life she built within the house maintains its certainties, even in widowhood, and she loves it still, the look of the fields beyond her, the quiet and peace of it. She is living in another kind of time from me: just these days, one after another, and I wonder what it is like for her to wake day after day into the drift of unspecified time. Sometimes her contentment makes me restless only because I can't imagine the same for myself: ambitionless time, time at its most elastic, almost shapeless. I depend on the hours at my desk, forming and re-forming experience and time, and I don't know what life would be without them. But my mother and I have our similarities. She has grown shy about the farm, and if I don't drop vegetables off on her porch, sometimes she'll buy apples and tomatoes at the supermarket even though Dave is growing them outside her door. It seems we are both ghosts.

4

ISLAND

And I have sent them a shell taken out of my well thirty-nine feet below the face of the earth, wrote Zacheus Macy of Nantucket in 1792, *and I have taken many sorts of shells out of wells near forty feet down. And one time when the old men were digging a well at the stage called Siasconset, it is said, they found a whale's bone near thirty feet below the face of the earth, which things are past our accounting for.* Geologists have long since proven those shells were the accretions of ice ages—layers, in turn, of the vestiges of warm-water life that had burgeoned in mild times, and of cold-water whelks and barnacles that made their way down from the north in advance of the ice. After the last glacier stopped and melted, it left a rough scatter of debris—the moraine—most of which was eventually drowned by a rising sea so that beneath the southernmost stretch of the Gulf of Maine lie the shoals ships must always navigate, and the land that has not yet drowned remains as the spine and low heights and sand plains of a chain of islands—Long Island, Martha's

Vineyard, Nantucket—Nantucket, nearly thirty miles off the New England coast, being the one that reaches farthest into the ocean, its tangled life accruing at the incremental pace insisted upon by salt and wind, its cliffs, spits, and reaches changing shape with every driven wave and storm.

When I think of the island, twenty years after having lived there, I often see myself walking through the heart of it. What was—and still is—the rough till deposited by the glacier had once been known as hunting grounds, then grazing grounds, and is now called the Moors: a low rolling landscape of scrub oak and pitch pine, bayberry, blueberry, pasture rose, grasses, mosses, false heather. Plants and animals abundant there are often rare beyond it, and sometimes strange. An owl hunts by day. Lady's slippers, those woodland orchids, thrive in sunlight. Always, there's the unmitigated sky. During my time summer houses had not yet been built on high places on the Moors, so often as I walked on the rutted dirt roads that crossed them I couldn't see a human structure. I had no sense of scale, and could believe, at the center of an island three miles wide and fifteen miles long, that I was in the midst of a vast heath. The roads themselves seemed to have no larger destination than a cranberry bog or one of the ponds—the kettle holes, where ice had once lingered after most of the glacier had melted back—and often they led only onto other roads, unpurposeful, and perfect for a dreaming mind. I wasn't the only one to see it as such: when artists paint and photograph the Moors these days they hardly ever represent humans in the works save for an occasional solitary gazer, as if it were entirely a place for onlookers, an immense consolation, an answer to desire. Though perhaps not for everyone: "It's like roaming an empty jail," I once heard someone say.

The landscape stood in absolute contrast to the inland world I had long known, and during my years in it I felt there was nothing attached to my own history, that I'd found a world I was utterly free to carve into, full of possibilities, a place to find my intended life. I remember feeling, upon leaving college, that I could go anywhere, though without some restriction on the possibilities—no other, no professional calling—I had no real idea of where to go. I'd settled on Nantucket because some friends lived on the island. I can see me there still, waiting at the ferry dock for my first crossing on a cold March morning, just a few boats at anchor in the harbor at Woods Hole. The land was gray, as was the sea, but you just knew the closedown was about to lift and a bit of green would be breaking out soon. My books, clothes, and little else were packed in a few soft bags slung over a bicycle. That's all I carried with me, that and a wish to become a writer, though I'd no idea at all of how to accomplish such a thing.

Very soon after settling into life on the island I discovered the Moors for what I hope they'll always be to me. Sometimes when I walked there under that sky I'd feel vulnerable to the exposure, especially when I saw another person in the distance, but more often I had a feeling of being out of reach and exposed only to immensity, as aloof and surveying as Henry Moore's *King and Queen*, that stoic sculpture he planted on the Scottish uplands. His idea for the work had begun as he was idly playing with a piece of modeling wax, which came first to resemble the head of Pan. *Then it grew a crown, and I recognized it immediately as the head of a king*, Moore had said. By the time of the sculpture's completion he had created two figures side by side whose delicate, complex heads appear graceful and intent on the vastness in front of them. *The land-*

scape is so bleak and impressive, so lacking in frilly bits of detail, so monumental, Moore had said of that heath. *The light is always changing too . . . The open air dwarfs everything because you relate it to the sky which is fathomless, endless, and to distance, which can be enormous.* For all the refinement of their heads, the rooted, weighty lower bodies of his sculpture seem to grow into the earth—or to emerge from it. The airy heads, the stolid feet somehow hold equal sway so you don't really know where power resides. Walking on the Moors was like that, making you feel both lifted and earthbound.

When the Wampanoag alone inhabited the island, the Moors had been their hunting grounds—after a good rain I sometimes found arrowheads that had washed onto the roads. The Indians had prospered longer on Nantucket than on the mainland coast: early epidemics hadn't reached them, and white settlement came relatively late to the island. Nantucket's Wampanoag population even grew a bit as other Indians, in flight from colonial settlement, arrived. They had cultivated cornfields on parts of the island, and as for the Moors, it's likely they burned them to keep the growth down for choice hunting—they had been so successful at the hunt that deer had been just about decimated by the seventeenth century. Such burning would have given the low-growing heathland and grassland vegetation breathing space to develop free of competition from larger plants for sunlight and for nutrients.

With the arrival in 1659 of the first white settler, Thomas Macy, the different understanding of land use and possession that the colonial world always brought with it came to Nantucket. Macy had left his established life at the mouth of the Merrimack River on the coastal plain above Boston after hav-

ing provoked the ire of the Puritan governors the year before
by giving shelter to some Quakers during a rainstorm, though
even prior to the incident he had been looking for a way to establish a settlement beyond Puritan control, and the island
presented a distinct possibility for resettlement since it wasn't
under any colonial jurisdiction. It may be true that settling an
island thirty miles out to sea was not, comparably, such an
enormous undertaking in the middle of the seventeenth century, when roads scarcely penetrated the densely wooded interior of Massachusetts and settlement still hugged the coast,
when water was a common means of travel. Although
Thomas Macy needed a man who knew the local waters to
help him navigate the shoals around the island, it would have
been less difficult for him to reach Nantucket than to breach
the inland frontier. Nantucket may, at that time, have felt
closer to the north coast of Boston than it would centuries
later, when the inland world was joined to the coast by road
and then rail, though you still had to travel to the island by
wooden ship and canvas sail.

Still, it unsettles me to think of him leaving all that he had
established for such an unknown—after all, Macy's life on the
mainland could hardly have been called insufferable. He'd
owned significant fertile, well-drained acreage in an agricultural world. One historian, in looking back at the settlement
of Nantucket, speculated that Macy and his fellow founders
were dreaming of re-creating the landscape they'd left behind
in England: *The open talk that boomed Nantucket would
not have been: "Macy and Starbuck and others are anxious
to get away to some outland where a man can think as he
chooses . . ." Rather it was: ". . . There are tidy little fortunes,
folks say, to be made there in cattle and sheep. Land much*

like the Devonshire commons, and the Wiltshire grazing runs." To dream such a thing in a new world is something other than a longing to re-create the past. It's also a longing for a past free from the past, for the appearance of grazing runs and commons without the confinements of a long-settled world. Maybe what D. H. Lawrence had claimed for the earliest settlers, whose desires for possession were marked by cattle and fencing and fields, was also true for Nantucket's first colonists: *Liberty in America has meant so far the breaking away from* all *dominion. The true liberty will only begin when Americans discover* IT, *and proceed possibly to fulfil* IT. IT *being the deepest* whole *self of man, the self in its wholeness, not idealistic halfness . . . We cannot see that invisible winds carry us, as they carry swarms of locusts, that invisible magnetism brings us as it brings the migrating birds to their unforeknown goal. But it is so. We are not the marvellous choosers and deciders we think we are.* IT *chooses for us, and decides for us . . . [I]f we are living people, in touch with the source,* IT *drives us and decides us.*

Macy's division of the island into an agricultural world—pasture, tillage, home—established the old Indian hunting grounds in the midst of the island as the Sheep Commons: the twenty original settlers each received a share, and the fourteen artisans—the coopers and wheelwrights and carpenters who came with them—each received a half share. A share consisted of 720 sheep commons; one sheep common was equal to an acre and a half, which would furnish pasture for one sheep or, alternatively, four geese. Each shareholder was allowed to keep the number of animals his share could support. A shareholder could keep one cow for every eight sheep commons held, and one horse for every sixteen. With no wolves on the island, there was no need for fencing. Each sheep was earmarked and roamed freely. On occasion animals wandered into town, and through the open doors of houses.

In the ensuing centuries, as the island moved from an agricultural world to one that followed the whaling trade farther and farther out to sea, the sheep continued to nibble away at the heathlands. The herd might diminish—during the meager times of the American Revolution it fell to no more than 3,000 sheep—but it was not to disappear until the nineteenth century. At times there were 15,000 sheep scattered across the moraine and the outwash plain. Their grazing, in addition to the constant salt spray and the poor quality of the soil, helped to keep the shrubs and small trees down, and so encouraged the heathland plants, just as fire may have in Indian times.

Cultivation changes the world and the light that falls on the world. René Dubos suggests something of how complex is the relationship between the human and wild when he considers the exploited landscape of Greece: *The humanization of the Greek wilderness has been achieved at great ecological loss.* At the same time he speculates: *While visiting the Moni Kaisarianis monastery, I noticed a dark opaque zone on the slopes of Mount Hymettus; this area had been reforested with pines. To me, it looked like an inkblot on the luminous landscape, especially at sunset, when the subtle violet atmosphere suffuses the bare rocks throughout the mountain range. The "divine illumination" lost much of its magic where it was absorbed by the pine trees . . . Not only did removal of the trees permit the growth of sun-loving aromatic plants and favor the spread of honeybees, as Plato had recognized; more importantly, it revealed the underlying architecture of the area and perhaps helped the soaring of the human mind.*

Nantucket, more northerly, surrounded by the cold green Atlantic, the snow-and-starred winters, produces a more brooding light on its once-grazed lands.

As the sheep were cropping the middle of the island, keeping open a place for the heathland plants, elsewhere under the plow the quality of the soils quickly declined. Early accounts had attested to the worth of the soil: *When first settled by the English, the soil was good and produced equal to any part of the country . . . Ebenezer Barnard, a man of strict veracity, in the year 1729, tilled five acres in the general cornfield, at that time on the north side of the island, between the Long Pond, so called, and the west end of the town, a tract of land below the medium quality. From these five acres he gathered 250 bushels of good corn, and this quantity was considered rather less than average for that year's growth. This may be accounted an uncommon growth for any country . . . In the year 1773, the cornfield was at Madaket and Smith's Point, at the northwesterly part of the island. The land then produced 20 bushels, on average, to the acre, which was considered a remarkably good crop. Since that time the crops have gradually lessened, and within a few years they would not average more than 10 or 15 bushels to the acre.*

I think of Nantucket, in a way, as the intensification of New England's agricultural fate. All through the Northeast in the eighteenth century fertility and topsoil were being lost to erosion and poor agricultural practices, but on Nantucket, with the winds off the water, with the exposure and salt, the effects were exacerbated: *At the time of the settlement of the island it was covered with wood, which protected the crops from the raw easterly winds, and by a continued supply of falling leaves and other decaying vegetation preserved the richness of the soil. The frequent ploughing of the land, since it was cleared of trees, has exposed the soil to the action of bleak winds, to which the island is very subject, and by which it is blown into the sea.* The soil had undergone so much degradation by the time of the American Revolution that Nantucketers—who numbered five thousand then—could not support themselves on the land: *The soil will not produce a subsistence for one third part of the people. Wholly destitute of fire wood and but a little clothing, such being their situation and circumstances . . . there will many people perish for want, before the end of another winter.*

The degradation of the soil had been so exacerbated by the loss of woodlands that the island was to become, in Herman Melville's words, *a mere hillock, and elbow of sand; all beach, without a background. There is more sand there than you would use in twenty years as a substitute for blotting paper. Some gamesome wights will tell you that they have to plant weeds there, they don't grow naturally; that they import Canada thistles; that they have to send beyond seas for a spile to stop a leak in an oil cask; that pieces of wood in Nantucket are carried about like bits of the true cross in Rome.* At one point in the nineteenth century, during a particularly cold winter, wood grew so scarce that islanders dismantled and burned two houses for warmth.

If with its salt- and wind-stunted vegetation the island had pulled itself even further away from the mainland, and from what the New England eye had grown used to, Nantucketers themselves seemed to be pulling away from the deemed character of New England, even in the way they kept their sheep: *The island being owned and improved in common, the sheep have not had that attention in the winter, which it is the general practice of farmers in the country to give to them. They are suffered to run at large throughout the year, exposed in winter to the bleak winds and cold storms, with no place of shelter provided for them. The forest has disappeared, and the greatest part of the island is left a naked plain, where the gale meets with no obstruction and animals find no refuge. It sometimes happens that many sheep are covered in heavy falls of snow, and perish before relief can be afforded, though large numbers of men are employed to release them. This mode of keeping sheep may to some appear wrong and even cruel; but it may be observed that the proprietors have always been in that practice, and, by long custom, have become so reconciled to the measure, that the thought of doing wrong has almost become extinct.*

Later writers would imagine that the separation from the mainland had been a profound one from the start. J. Hector St. John de Crèvecœur, upon seeing Nantucket in the last half of the eighteenth century, saw a place that in no way resembled the cultivated farmland of the mainland, and could not imagine that those who first settled the island were dreaming of grazing runs, or that its barrenness had been something exacerbated by settlement. He understood Thomas Macy's settlement of the island in a particular light: *Who would have imagined that any people should have abandoned a fruitful and extensive continent, filled with the riches which the most ample vegetation affords, replete with good soil, enamelled meadows, rich pastures, every kind of timber, and with all other materials necessary to render life happy and comfortable, to come and inhabit a little sand-bank, to which nature had refused those advantages; to dwell on a spot where there scarcely grew a shrub to announce, by the budding of its leaves, the arrival of spring . . .* And he ascribed to the first founders an intent they may not have had to begin with: *They found it so universally barren, and so unfit for cultivation, that they mutually agreed not to divide it, as each could neither live on, nor improve, that lot which might fall to his share. They then cast their eyes on the sea . . .*

The Whale Fishery had begun as a source of supplementary income, with the stripping of pilot whales that had washed up on the beaches. The pilot whales' element, like the mariner's, is the deep, but sometimes they follow the squid near shore. They navigate by sounding, and the shifting, sandy bottoms of the old moraine can confuse them. They become like birds caught in a cage. Pilot whales move in pods, and when they become disoriented dozens can become stranded at one time. It was this tendency to beach in numbers that made shore whaling attractive to the early colonists. By the late seventeenth century it was so widely practiced that appointed inspectors decided whose property the beached whales were. The discoverer received a third share, the colonial government a third, the town a third.

Eventually men began to pursue whales in the local waters: *When they come within our harbors, boats surround them. They are as easily driven to the shore as cattle or sheep are driven on land. The tide leaves them, and they are easily killed. They are a fish of the whale kind, and will average a barrel of oil each. I have seen nearly four hundred at one time lying dead on the shore.* Nantucketers understood the rich potential of the harvest early on. Historian Obed Macy recounts, *In the year 1690 . . . some persons were on a high hill, afterwards called Folly House Hill, observing the whales spouting and sporting with each other, when one observed "there," pointing to the sea, "is a green pasture where our children's grandchildren will go for bread."*

The sea can be understood as prairie, the human adventure on it taken up in the manner of any other cultivation. Like medieval villagers moving beyond their bounds, carving a bit more from the wilderness as their plows and animals improved and the population grew, over time men pursued different kinds of whales in more distant waters. After a while, there was no returning from the sea at the end of the day. The hours on the hunt became days, then seasons, until whalers were spending years sailing to the South Pacific in search of the sperm whale. The sailors became more and more separate from life onshore. The Nantucketer became entirely peculiar. Herman Melville was to write, . . . *these sea hermits issuing from their ant-hill in the sea, overrun and conquered the watery world like so many Alexanders; parcelling out among them the Atlantic, Pacific, and Indian oceans . . . [T]wo thirds of this terraqueous globe are the Nantucketer's. . . . For years he knows not the land; so that when he comes to it at last it smells like another world, more strangely than the moon would to an Earthsman. With the landless gull, that at sunset folds her wings and is rocked to sleep between billows; so at nightfall, the Nantucketer, out of sight of land, furls his sails, and lays him to his rest, while under his very pillow rush herds of walruses and whales.*

By the nineteenth century whaling ships were sharing the seas with countless other craft: wooden ships under canvas sail carried immigrants, travelers, cargoes of seeds, cattle, sheep, paving stones, furniture. Most captains navigated near land by coasting—shadowing the shore from one landmark to the next. Sometimes the only passage from one place to another was over shoals. In a stretch of quiet summer weather the changes in them might be almost imperceptible, but sandy shoals—embryonic lands that have not yet broken through the sea's surface, old lands dead, dying, onetime islands long since become rumor—may change shape faster than the navigation charts can be revised. In winter, in rough weather, spits can wash away overnight. Points become islands, islands become spits. Nineteenth-century ships lost steering, there were fires on board. They had no long-range forecasts. The lighthouses, with their oil lamps, could fail in the worst weather. A lightship might run off course. When the lights failed there was the foghorn, but sound bends on the wind, in the water and fog. You can't get your bearings by it. It can only let you know that you are near. If you are lost for a moment you could be lost for good, even in our sea, so sounded and certain, read from the air and scanned by radar, its currents tracked and mapped. A storm surge puts every mariner back into the world Melville charted: *In that gale, the port, the land, is that ship's direst jeopardy; she must fly all hospitality; one touch of land, though it but graze the keel, would make her shudder through and through. With all her might she crowds all sail off shore; in so doing, fights 'gainst the very winds that fain would blow her homeward; seeks all the lashed sea's landlessness again.*

Thoreau, on Cape Cod, observed, . . . *and sometimes more than a dozen wrecks are visible from this point at one time. The inhabitants hear the crash of vessels going to pieces as they sit round their hearths, and they commonly date from some memorable shipwreck.* Each wreck had its society: there would be those who worked to aid the dead and the near dead, a few would go on collecting nearby seaweed that the storm had washed in, others scavenged what remained of the ship, or were on the watch for whatever valuables the tide brought in: turnip seed, barrels of apples, scrap iron, wood, books, ties . . . The coastal world, both the cultivated and the wild, could seem to be half built out of flotsam. *Another . . . showed me, growing in his garden, many pear and plum trees which washed ashore . . . all nicely tied up and labeled,* Thoreau remarked during his journey on the Cape. He also heard of a man who saw *something green growing in the pure sand of the beach, just at high-water mark, and on approaching found it to be a bed of beets flourishing vigourously, probably from seed washed out of the Franklin.* Whatever the profit, there was always a loss: *When I remarked to an old wrecker partially blind, who was sitting on the edge of the bank smoking a pipe, which he had just lit with a match of dried beach-grass, that I supposed he liked to hear the sound of the surf, he answered: "No I do not like to hear the sound of the surf."* He had lost at least one son in "the memorable gale," and could tell many a tale of the shipwrecks which he had witnessed there.

There had been, by the mid-nineteenth century, so many wrecks and deaths in the coastal waters that eventually, especially along the sandy shores—the granite shoals, after all, proved more constant—the Humane Society placed huts on the desolate reaches: *The traveler stands for example on the southern shore of the island of Nantucket, and after looking off over the boundless ocean which stretches in that direction without limit or shore for thousands of miles, and upon the*

surf rolling in incessantly on the beach, whose smooth ex-
panse is dotted here and there with the skeleton remains of
ships that were lost in former storms, and are now half buried
in the sand, he sees, at length, a hut, standing upon the shore
just above the reach of the water—the only human structure
to be seen. He enters the hut. The surf boat is there, resting
upon its rollers, all ready to be launched, and with its oars
and all its furniture and appliances complete, and ready for
the sea. The fireplace is there, with the wood laid, and
matches ready for the kindling. Supplies of food and clothing
are also at hand—and a compass: and on a placard, conspicu-
ously posted, are the words: SHIPWRECKED MARINERS REACH-
ING THIS HUT, IN FOG OR SNOW, WILL FIND THE TOWN OF
NANTUCKET TWO MILES DISTANT, DUE WEST. I imagine it
open-mouthed facing the sea, not a harbor or village in sight,
just the solitary house that will save ten or one or seven sur-
vivors.

The edge of the sea attracts people looking for a definite limit,
and freedom. Twenty-some years ago, anyway, the island was
a place you could tuck into for a while, not too obvious
among the descendants of the first founders—the Coffins and
Macys—and the Portuguese from the Azores descended from
the whalers, the summer people turned permanent, artists and
writers—the complex of communities that make up many
shifting coastal towns now that tourism rather than fishing is
the mainstay. The human community there has as many small
and competing interests as the heath, and it has more in common with the sandy shoals than it knows.

Nantucket felt more apart from anything I had ever
known, and that apartness sometimes helped with definition.

Others were "from away." I was "from away" to others on the island, I know, though I told myself my life was tucked up enough so I wasn't really noticed. I loved its closeness, and it would be years before I found it confining. There was still a place for sidetracked life, for people who didn't mind being the last one, though even then you could see in the increasing affluence of the town how those who had once been ordinary people in the community were becoming characters, and might soon become nuisances to the idea of the place. I was grateful for the way the island allowed me to travel my own hidden path while I nursed my hopes of becoming a writer, and also afforded me a bit of protection from the expectant eyes of my family.

During my first years on the island my attempts at writing were sporadic, and I told myself the distractions were the stuff of life—I was busy with friends and work in restaurants and bookstores, work that paid my rent—but my failure to make headway weighed on me so much that I began to look for a way to impose greater discipline on myself. One winter three years after having arrived there, I agreed to house-sit on the Squam Road, a rutted dirt track that ran between the swamp and the sea on the eastern edge of Nantucket. I thought by putting myself farther away on the island I could find enough solitude and silence to begin writing in earnest. The winter landscape of Squam felt utterly wild: bayberry, swamp oak, black alder—gray, grayer, grayest—were all stunted by poor soil and salt and gnarled by the wind. Everything had long been growing into everything else, and had become impenetrable to humans, crossed over by deer paths, eyed by marsh hawks on their wavering, tipping wings. I don't think there was anyone else living on the Squam Road that winter—at least I never saw a light except the one I left on for myself.

Most of the gray-shingled houses that faced the open ocean, their windows washed and stained with salt spray, had been built for summer.

Even now I think I should have named that wind, and added it to the list of legendary winds of the world—the foehn and the mistral, the chinook and the Santa Ana—though it was a private wind that didn't seem to reach anyone but me as it blew steadily in from the Atlantic. All winter long it blew, and it came up most fiercely after the sudden twilights that ushered in the long nights in a world going down into winter. It defined my walls and windows and made the house creak and bray as it rushed across my unformed life and then across the tangled scrub of the swamp. I had never feared the wind the way I did then, on nights so dark I couldn't see my hand in front of my face, and the bright, polished stars were so many they weighed down on me, much as I wanted to be able to stand and stare, to remark with matter-of-fact wonder: *one could not have put a finger in between them.* The darkness seemed to compound the fury of the wind, and all of it would have driven me crazy if I hadn't lit a large fire every night, stacking log upon log in the brick fireplace. When the creaking and braying cut especially deep, I'd crash more logs onto the flames and sleep right beside it, curled in my blankets, solitary daughter of those who were never to ask for help, of sturdy inland souls whose voices I imagined hearing during those nights. *Keep at it,* they'd said. *Use your head.*

Maybe it's true that the greater part of my fear was simply of being alone on that road, and a woman alone having to face her own life, but I don't think that could have been everything. For all its beauty, and however much I loved it by day—the inlets and salt creeks, the beach rose, the red berries of the black alder shining out of the swamp oak—I was also

bewildered by a terrain that was so different from those water-
worn hills north of Boston, where wilderness was kept at bay
by cultivated rows and furrows. I think now I was most afraid
of an absolutely unbounded world, and me silent and singular
within it. As I remember the fires, those stars, that wind, it
seems as if it was all a part of being tested, and having failed.

Still, when I sat down to work in the mornings as the sky
lightened over the Atlantic and the wind calmed for a while, I
remember having an unusual amount of energy, not only from
the sheer relief at having gotten through the night but also
from attempting to begin what I'd longed for. I loved the day-
time there in unusual proportion, loved the feeling of being at
absolute sea level, the density in the sea air, the dampness and
thickness of it. Absent the night wind, a stunning, palpable
quiet surrounded me as I worked, while beyond the window,
as daylight slowly silvered the swamp, the uncultivated landscape of Squam grew more and more distinct.

If I think of Squam long enough, I remember the fires of that
April, too, when the days were more insistent than the nights,
and the wind had a warmth to it, and a fragrance, and lost
much of its power over me. I'd sit in the front doorway and
bask in the mild dusk and the first red energy of spring while
behind me—half in my view, half forgotten—the last split oak
of the year burned gently in the fireplace. Those nights I fell
asleep easily as the foghorns sounded one after another across
shrouded water. Though the mildness of the new season was
strong enough to allay my fears, my winter in Squam turned
out to mark my last year on the island. I had created for myself a greater discipline and focus, and the accomplishment
seemed to create a new restlessness in me. I found myself

wanting more of the world than the island, even with its vast sky, could provide. My arrival four years earlier may have been a questioning of what I was aiming for; to leave was a questioning again—all leavings are a questioning of what is left behind, the eternal questions of immigration. To leave is to want change, however much you may want what is left behind somehow to remain the same.

I wanted a correction for the remoteness of those years, a place more in the thick of things, so I settled into an apartment outside Boston. For the longest time I felt shy of the world at large, and I couldn't quite believe I wouldn't be returning to the island. When fog settled around my apartment, I was disoriented without the low warnings of foghorns. I remember walking down the streets thinking I couldn't get enough air. The air wasn't dense enough: Squam air had an almost solid weight. Outside the double-decker where I lived, human energy was everywhere palpable, and the streets were always busy, even after a snow. Before the last flakes had fallen the shovelers were out in full force, and the sand trucks and plows moved through in formation, clearing every last bit away. The cars going by sounded as if they were driving through rain. I was overwhelmed, even as I knew I had left Squam partly for fear of growing too far away from all the noise of life. Or that's how I put it to myself, anyway. And still sometimes I dreamt of the world I had had to myself, and what I remembered as the immense quiet of it all. Sometimes I chastised myself for not having loved those solitary nights when I could.

I must have been after that same sense of silence and solitude I'd experienced in Squam when, nearly fifteen years later, I decided to build a working space separate from my home on the farm. My small house was feeling noisy by then: it sits on a slight rise and is oriented toward what these days is a busy commuter road, and away from the unperturbed life of the apple orchard. There had been only a few small windows giving onto that back view, just large enough to let some sun through, enough to peer out at the winter shadows stretching early and long across the snow, the house shadow blending with the shadows of those cragged apple trees, which blend with those of the high white pines of the woods beyond as the last light lingers in the treetops a hundred feet above.

The house has an old shed attached to it which had been built seventy-five years before, from salvaged barn timbers. All kinds of nails and rusted hooks hang from the walls; the wood has long gone brown with age. The rear of it slopes toward the orchard, and I began to imagine a room carved out of the back which would look out on those trees. It would have to be a room turned around from the practical, with half the windows facing north. I thought I could keep much of the shed intact—just shore up some timbers and raise a few walls—but the carpenter said squaring it would be too costly, and the most he could do was save the old beams. He cut a full third of the shed away and built me an entirely new room: full of windows, white, spare, square, true, and how I love that back view.

In winter when I lift my eyes from work and look straight into the measured rows of the orchard—without blossoms or leaves, without the spring haze of incipience—I see thickened trunks and branches trained to resilient strength and spareness by years of pruning. You'll know them if you've seen Mondrian's *The Grey Tree* painted an ocean away, nearly a century ago, just before he moved into pure abstraction. His gray limbs sprout branches that catch the turbulent and dense gray air and finally thin into the merest slips that are caught by the air, even as they cut it. They seem to stand for all the contending forces in the world. Mondrian, who in later life, when asked why he was reworking his earlier canvases, said, *I don't want pictures. I just want to find things out.*

When my work goes well I'm surrounded by the same palpable silence I remember from Squam. In my study—larger than any room in my house, lower, brighter—days go by and papers and books pile up around the edges of my desk, crowding me into a world of its own accretion, with its own absorption and fidelity. It's not far from Squam in its hopes still, though the days are accompanied by greater discipline, and the pencil and paper I used on that table twenty years ago have given way to the whirs and grunts of a Macintosh. *[T]here has to be,* writes Adrienne Rich, *an imaginative transformation of reality which is in no way passive. And a certain freedom of the mind is needed—freedom to press on, to enter the currents of your thought like a glider pilot, knowing that your motion can be sustained, that the buoyancy of your attention will not be suddenly snatched away. Moreover, if the imagination is to transcend and transform experience it has to question, to challenge, to conceive of alternatives, perhaps to the very life you are living at that moment. You have to be free to play around with the notion that day might be night, love might be hate; nothing can be too sacred for the imagination to turn into its opposite or to call experimentally by another name. For writing is re-naming.*

Such a world is inexplicable in its richness and its costs, and creates in you a more solitary creature than you might otherwise have been. Or it may meet your own solitary nature. I know when I walk out into the day, that interior I've left behind can seem matchless and inarticulate even to myself, never mind to others working on the outside. And yet the reality of the open day seems to depend so much on those stowed-away hours. *I am here alone for the first time in weeks, to take up my "real" life again at last,* wrote May Sarton. *That is what is strange—that friends, even passionate love, are not my real life unless there is time alone in which to explore and to discover what is happening or has happened. Without the interruptions, nourishing and maddening, this life would become arid. Yet I taste it fully only when I am alone here and "the house and I resume old conversations."*

Every once in a while my work is unnerving—flat or obdurate—and I have the same old feeling of being tested and having failed that I endured during those wind-compounded nights on the island. Then I go back into the inch-deep solace of my house and sit down at the dining room table to work. Easier, I tell myself, with the swish of cars going by on the road and the juncos pecking at seeds in the snow, the kettle whistling and the splash of last summer's geraniums brought in, their sharp scent come to life by the heat of the wood burning in the stove.

I still have some old friends living on the island, and I like to go down for a fall or winter visit—never in summer with the crowds, not if I can help it. In recent years, even in winter the island has come to feel much less remote to me. Maybe that has something to do with the greater number of houses and people, or with how quickly you can get there now on the ferry, but I think it might have as much to do with my mere dipping into that world. You need to dwell in a place for a good while before its true remoteness sinks in and moves in your imagination. All I know is that as the boat nears the island I still habitually move to its port side so as to look out at Coatue, the barrier beach that protects the harbor from the sound. It's just a spit of sand with grasses and some scrub, so low you can believe it might sometimes be washed over by tides. It seems as vulnerable and beautiful as always, but it used to mark more for me, as I came and went during the years I lived there, as the winter ferry slipped past so early in the morning, the sun rising behind Monomoy, the engine humming, the boat quiet with passengers dozing on their coats or sipping coffee. Our voices never seemed to gain strength until we passed all land and were well into the sound. Nantucket had mattered so much to me for a handful of years. It had been difficult to leave. Now to see Coatue vulnerable and beautiful as ever, and not to be stung by longing, is its own sadness.

The island itself seems conscious of its own rapid change, and unable to slow it. Sometimes when I stop to chat with old acquaintances in the street they ask if I've been out to Squam.

"No, no, not yet."

"Don't go. You won't recognize it." The summer houses have gotten bigger, they say, and there are so many more of them. It might be true that in summer or on an unseasonably mild off-season day I wouldn't recognize the place, but I'd like to believe that even if there are three or four lights on the Squam Road now as the January sun goes down, I'd know it for what it always was on those winter nights.

When Nantucket remembers itself it remembers itself as a whaling town thrumming with the work of coopers and smiths and stitchers at work in the sail lofts, a town smelling of the tryworks, like *the left wing of the day of judgement*, though that world had burned to the ground in the nineteenth century, and sand sifted into the harbor mouth and silted it up and made the passage of larger ships untenable. The whale fishery became concentrated in New Bedford even as the gold rush was sending desiring imaginations elsewhere and the advent of kerosene had begun to swamp the whale oil industry. Still, the more time passes, the more established becomes the remembrance of that world. The historical association, long a healthy presence in town, is planning to expand its museum to include a whale oil and candle factory as well as the 1850 Fresnel lens from the Sankaty Lighthouse and the full skeleton of a sperm whale that washed up on the beach a few years ago.

These days when the pilot whales beach themselves on the Cape and islands there is an outpouring of concern along with enduring curiosity. When more than fifty of them drifted onto the shores of the outer Cape a few summers ago, the event made national news for a week. Vacationers came out by the hundreds in a frantic effort to lead them back to sea. Once the pilot whales are out of their element, though, their own weight begins to crush their internal organs. Their skin burns and blisters in the sun. While people waited for the tide to haul them back out, they covered them with wet towels and bedsheets, and schoolchildren carried buckets of water to pour on them. A photo from the air makes the scene look almost like a carnival, with all the bright colors of their clothes and paraphernalia. Eventually, several men guided each whale back out beyond the surf, but getting beyond the surf was the least of it. Volunteers stood watch all through the evening and again at first light to see if the whales would return, and they inevitably did, being too exhausted to find their way to open water. There were more volunteers and less help for them with the second effort to get them back to sea. A third return. Even more died, and they died more quickly, until finally veterinarians euthanized the rest.

The sheep have been gone from the heart of the island for more than a century. They had grazed on until the island economy declined in the 1860s, when not only had whaling declined, cheaper wool from the west decreased local demand. After the grazing herds diminished, the heath began to lose its foothold, and it might have disappeared entirely under the growth of scrub oak and pitch pine had not residents, sometime later in the nineteenth century, begun to burn what they now called the Moors. The burning was meant to attract large flocks of American golden plovers and curlews, which were killed for market. As Fred Bosworth notes in *Last of the Curlews: And sometimes, during northeast storms, tremendous numbers of the curlews would be carried in from the Atlantic Ocean to the beaches of New England, where at times they would land in a state of great exhaustion, and they could be chased and easily knocked down with clubs when they attempted to fly. Often they alighted on Nantucket in such numbers that the shot supply of the island would become exhausted and the slaughter would have to stop until more shot could be secured from the mainland . . . The gunner's name for them was "dough-bird," for it was so fat when it reached us in the fall that its breast would often burst open when it fell to the ground, and the thick layer of fat was so soft that it felt like a ball of dough. It is no wonder that it was so popular as a game bird, for it must have made a delicious morsel for the table. It was so tame and unsuspicious and it flew in*

such dense flocks that it was easily killed in large numbers . . .
Two Massachusetts market gunners sold $300 worth from
one flight . . . Boys offered the birds for sale at 6 cents apiece
. . . In 1882 two hunters on Nantucket shot 87 Eskimo
curlew in one morning . . . By 1894 there was only one
dough-bird offered for sale on the Boston market.

The burnings stopped when the birds disappeared, open-
ing the heath once more to competition from scrubby oaks
and pines. In recent years conservationists, in order to encour-
age the heathland habitat, have attempted to replicate the effects of grazing and old fires by performing controlled burns.
Sometimes you can detect in the effort a desire for purity, for
a world before our own design. *We have built roads, which*
stop the spread of fires, and extinguished fires that would
have burned prior to European settlement, one scientist com-
mented. *We have built houses and planted trees that interrupt*
the salt spray. We are not letting nature take its course.

I had taken for granted, when I walked on the Moors, that I
was walking on free space, and there was nothing stopping
me from striking out long and far. It was one of the few un-
marked places where I'd never been shadowed by a feeling of
trespass. I had no idea that shares of the Commons, as origi-
nally set out by Thomas Macy, were still owned and had been
divided and handed down through generations, diminished by
successive estates so that now bits of them were the property
of people spread out over the world. In modern times, if one
wants to buy or sell a parcel, one has to track down the scattered inheritors of the Commons, or prove the rightful owners
cannot be found. Developers do, as do the conservation or-
ganizations, which acquire land on the Moors just as aggres-

sively as they acquire shoreline in an effort to keep the bound-aries of the island as it has been known, and the growth of the Moors as they have been known. NO MOOR HOUSES, the bumper stickers said when I was there.

There were Moor houses, of course. Nantucket became more prosperous through the 1980s and 1990s, and execu-tives built large summer homes even on the part of the moraine that had once been known as hunting grounds, then grazing grounds. The town itself seems to work toward that prosperity the way the old Nantucket town had worked toward whaling. More and more of the island people sell houses, or work for the moneyed, keeping and building houses in support of that trade. There aren't enough ordinary people on the island to fill certain demands now that the cost of housing has risen beyond the reach of the island's children and the laborers. Carpentry crews fly in daily from the main-land.

The five-and-dime store and the modest department store on Main Street have gone out of business. Many storefronts display beautiful decorative wares from central Italy and southern France, but you have to search off-island to buy things for daily life. Sometimes wedding guests lining the church steps open envelopes stuffed with live butterflies as the bride and groom depart after their vows. Controversies flare over four-wheel-drive rights to beach access, and traffic ties up Main Street all summer long. Still, the Moors possess a scent all their own, nothing like the sea, nothing like *the left wing of the day of judgement.* When I catch the scent I some-times imagine that, in supporting a rare habitat, the nibbling mouths of sheep may have had a more lasting impact than the leviathan, and that the bayberry, with its heady oils, having grown on long after the grazing has stopped, will make a candle to light a smaller, more intimate world than whale oil ever illuminated.

I can't imagine my factual understanding of Nantucket ever being clearer than it is now, the way it has been measured and mapped and studied under glass, so much more certain than when Zaccheus Macy puzzled out the bones and shells he took from wells. Even so, it is a place that can't be fixed by the clearest photo taken from space, in which the Atlantic shows itself as an even expanse of oceanic blue while long-established lands stand resolutely green against the drab gray and beige of human settlements. The ground grains of fossil and stone that make up the shoreline show white and appear cauterized to a permanence, as if the edge of land could ever be so crisp and stilled. The photo suggests nothing of the way the sands shift and change with every tide and gale, now losing ground to the sea as the sands absorb the power of a storm surge, now gaining ground as a quiet tide seeps in. On vast stretches of sandy coast there's nothing for shore life to cling to, and what survives survives by burrowing. *I was always aware that I was treading on the thin rooftops of an underground city,* Rachel Carson once wrote of walking along just such a shore. *Of the inhabitants themselves little or nothing was visible. There were the chimneys and stacks and ventilating pipes of underground dwellings, and various passages and runways leading down into darkness. There were little heaps of refuse that had been brought up to the surface as though in an attempt at some sort of civic sanitation. But the inhabitants remained hidden, dwelling silently in their dark, incomprehensible world.*

It is thought, from all the erosion and the inexorable rising of the sea, that the island may disappear completely in another three centuries, but for now, if I look at that photo long enough, my imagination puts Nantucket-as-seen-from-space in motion. Most everything else feels as if it comes under the pull of the mainland, the way Cape Cod curves inward to Massachusetts Bay, and the Vineyard leans into the Elizabeth Islands, while Nantucket appears intent on putting even more distance between itself and the mainland, the way Tom Nevers—its southeast headland—juts out. If Melville had seen it from space he would have thought of the brow of the whale itself, for it is every bit as blunt as the summit of Mount Greylock as seen from his hill-shrouded study window. I think first of the *Winged Victory of Samothrace* leading herself toward the open sea with the thrust of her torso. The northward points of Tuckernuck and Muskeget, and Great Point—those fragile spits of land—stream back like her wings, as if the island itself were in flight now that time is collapsing the distance between it and everything else. You can jet in from Boston in scant minutes, and the air above is full of engine noise, and the ferry across the sound goes twice as fast as it used to, getting you there in a perfect hour, hardly enough time to feel a sense of transgression or any singularity about the trip, however much I want to know it the way Melville imagined it—*away off shore, more lonely than the Eddystone lighthouse.* Surely its apartness must be the one constant in all its history. Surely something about Nantucket remains past accounting for.

5

GRANGE

Perhaps it's only that my father had no time for the sea and my mother was always dreaming of it, but sometimes I say *salt hay* to myself again and again for nothing beyond the pleasure of the slight discord I feel between the two words, discord of both sound and sense. *Salt*: the one curt syllable glints sharp and stinging. To stand at the headlands and smell it, however much you love the ocean, is to know there's no sheltered world. Steadily roaring breakers are constant in your ears, you gaze into an infinity, whatever weather moves out over the water and curls back contains a fierce and renewed strength. But *hay*, with its open *a*, is assuaging, and suggests an infinite calm: it belongs to an inland world, and lies at the heart of agriculture, for hay must always be made, and does not exist without human effort. Cultivation itself is a dream of shelter against the unpredictable, and essential to our dream of it is the sweet and redolent smell of cut grasses blooming and deepening on the air, then diminishing as the harvest dries and burnishes. In those marshes

alone, on the margin between land and sea, salt and hay shoal
one into the other, each word claiming the shifting boundaries
of both worlds. A scythe sweeps the grass, somewhere out beyond the surf a buoy bell clangs. *Have salt in yourselves,* says
Mark, *and have peace one with another.*

I would never have known a thing of the salt hay harvest
had I not seen Martin Johnson Heade's paintings where, under a nineteenth-century sky, looming haystacks—now gold
and gleaming, now in shadow—dominate the marshes. The
stacks might be twelve feet high—outsized, the way he's
painted them—and thatched so sturdily, without a waver or a
list, they appear every bit as stable as the land itself, as if
they'd never give in to gravity or wind, or drift onto the uplands in a stormy tide. They're larger than anything human.
Men move among them, men and boys dwarfed by what
they've made. Smaller, much smaller, among the stacks are a
few cattle scattered on the marsh, a cart of hay being taken to
the barn or up to the spreading grounds, some men raking in
the distance. Skies change—storms wash over the marsh, sun-
rise, sunset, twilight, a glaring orange sun, or diffused light
settling on everything—skies change, and the light that falls
on the land changes, but the world remains steady: the cattle
do not sink and need to be shot, the horses don't misstep and
break a leg, a man does not misjudge the tide and get caught
on the open water without a way back home.

It never existed, of course, a world of such constancy and
peace. Cattle did sink, and horses misstep, and in a rare instance a man would lose his life while haying, but the
marshes, and the human lives in their proximity, were inextricably tied to each other in the world Heade painted steadily
for more than forty years, mainly in the permutations of its

harvest season, leaving others to render the chasms and canyons of the frontier. What Heade painted was the last strong time of salt hay harvesting. The cutting of spartina, which had receded as the country expanded westward across the ranges and into the prairie, enjoyed a nineteenth-century revival when Northeast farms began to grow as the textile cities crowded in and the factories grew larger and farmers began to increase their herds to satisfy the demand for milk. They lacked adequate tillage land for their cows since many of the old fields had grown up into impenetrable thickets, then woods, but the salt marshes—the ones that hadn't been cut off from the sea by roads, or drained for development, or turned into cropland for corn, onions, and strawberries—remained open. Extremes, after all, have their own kind of stability: sometimes a different grass might have moved onto the marsh, but because of the salt, nothing of any stature—no cedar or pine, oak or hickory—had taken hold.

At the end of the nineteenth century those open marshes seemed more valuable than ever. *They used to tell you if you weren't sure of your bounds, you had better find out, for if you should cut over the line . . . you would be liable for damages*, one of the last to remember the salt hay harvest says. And: *They thought so much of that salt marsh hay, they would fight for the last spear.* Farmers brought down all they needed from higher ground and camped by the shore during harvest time. Along with scythes and rakes, they carried bog shoes for the horses so their animals could better maneuver the spongy earth. They used flat-bottom boats, called gundalows, to haul the cut grass up the creeks. As before, they built staddles out of old logs to stack the hay on so that it would stand above the wash of floods and tides. Tools born of a marginal, particular world, belonging to a limited place in time and to no other. *On the south side of the path was Frank Pevear mowing with one horse . . . I can see him now. He was walking behind the machine. Warren H. Batchelder doing the mowing with a two-horse mower . . . John N. Sanborn mowing his 23 acres with his own red roan horse. He walked back of the machine. Then, Stephen Brown mowing his own 11 acres. We could count around 30 horses and 60 men sometimes. Then in about two days or more when the mowing was finished, there would be just a few horses but around 100 men and boys, raking and stacking. There were lots more over toward the Hampton River and up west, back of the trees toward the Hampton Falls dock. In the September season it was the same thing but not so many boys.*

It must have seemed, even in the last long August days of it, with the switchel cooling in the ditch, and the horses' bog shoes white with salt, and stacks growing higher and higher, that it was a world certain of its footing: *I would like to tell you how we used to haul the hay to the stack . . . We made that drag. It worked so well there was no way to improve on it. You had to drive with long reins, standing on the short plank. The hay would slide up the side of that plank and keep going forward all the time and by the time it had gotten to the horse's heels, it would be piled up in front of you and out the sides against the ropes. There would be enough to call it a load . . .*

They knew how many days in the month the tide ran in the marshes. They knew the greenheads wouldn't bite in the shade, and that the mosquitoes were worse going down than on the marsh itself. They knew not to lay a scythe on the ground where a horse or a man might step on it. That it was a bad thing to be caught on the marsh without fresh water. They watched the moons and the tides, knowing you had to live with your judgments, and with whatever was gathering on the gray-blue sea strewn with whitecaps: *One afternoon he was going down to get a stack of hay . . . It was on a low run of tide but it seems that there was a bad storm at sea that no one knew about and the tide coming up. He was on the marsh when the tide started to come up but knowing that the tide was a low run he didn't think much of it. As the tide kept coming he decided to turn around and go back but before he got near shore the tide was so deep he could not see the path. He stopped. The hired man thought he knew the way and went on but became lost in the river and drowned. John Thayer stayed, standing up in the pung and holding his son all night.*

They could not improve on it, but neither could they save a passing way of life: in the end there was no way to compete with the larger farms and herds to the west, or the speed and economy of long-distance transport, or their children's dreams of other lives. The tide has rinsed the marshes countless times since those large harvests, and almost a century later I have found only one voice that fully remembered that world. John Fogg's written account is hidden away in the special collection of a coastal town's library: *They poled enough hay for the stack and I raked the scatterings. When they got the bottom started I layed the stack. When pitching they had to watch how the stack was being layed out over the staddle. The one on the stack had no way of telling how it was looking. They needed some more hay to make a good top. While they were out getting more, I had then a chance to look around and what a sight to see, all those doing the same as we were, stacking as far as the eye could see in all directions.*

Then, even a boy could build a haystack so solid that a weighted, tarred rope alone would protect it from autumn's storms and winds, so solid the memory of it might give an old man a foothold in a soft and noisy life where summer bathers—insubstantial in the shimmer of heat, smelling of sunscreen—face the open water, radios going. *That was the best part of the stacking, standing on the very top of the stack,* he remembers. And it seems he stands for a whole grounded world waiting for liftoff. It's sweltering in August. His face is flushed from work. Salt hay scratches at his eyes and throat. The sun goes in and out of high, fair clouds, and everything around him—the homes and home fields, the distinct salt sea, the marsh and its harvesters—is lit, in its turn, by the brilliance.

When I read John Fogg's account of salt haying, it was the scope as much as the work itself that drew me in— the world entire: *all those doing the same as we were.* A farm does need to be part of a world, not so different from the way an owl or even the common deer needs contiguous habitat— greenways, they are called—for survival. Now that agriculture is marginal here, a farmer might find himself traveling far to talk. "I go down to the gun show in Worcester, just to be around the fellows. They come from all over. A lot from the West—their places go on for days . . . You wouldn't believe it, they have tourists on the cattle drives now, taking the cows up to the summer pastures," one of my neighbors told me during an evening at the Grange. He went on: "Oh, how your father would love to hear that."

The Grange Hall still stands in the heart of our town, foursquare, muted and staid against the lit signs of the tanning salon beside it and the convenience store across the way. It's often dark except during the Monday evening meetings, the fall bake sale and yard sale, and the annual roast beef dinner. Most of the few dozen men and women who remain members of our local chapter have known one another all their lives, and have belonged since they were young. Up on the second story of the hall I've heard you can still read names carved into the rafters above the dance floor, which was said to be the finest in the lower valley for the way it would give under their stomping, kicking boots in the days when they flirted and tossed their partners—the Yankees whose ancestors had come over on the second sailing of the *Mayflower* mingling with the children of Poles, French Canadians, Greeks, Armenians, and Lebanese whose families had moved out of the cities to take over farms at the end of the nineteenth century.

There haven't been dances for decades. The largest gatherings are for the fall dinners, when we all contentedly eat thin-sliced beef, whipped squash, and green beans, and wash down the apple and lemon meringue pies with hot coffee. Henry Clough, who still keeps a straggling orchard that crests the top of one of the hills, is too blind to drive anymore, so he comes with Agimah, the foreman of his Jamaican apple-picking crew, and Agimah eats silently in our midst, a whole head above us, spine straight, not looking to his left or right, helping himself to seconds and thirds, while at his shoulders men and women cough and clear their throats and talk on about the old days. Most don't farm full time anymore (the younger farmers who do don't have time for the Grange).

Their hay no longer feeds dairy herds, but is a fragmented commodity shipped out across southern New England to area racetracks and horse stables. Bales of the lesser grades are used by the construction industry as a buffer between work projects and wetlands, or for lawn decorations in the fall, or garden mulch. When I see trucks laden on the highways I imagine a field condensed and moving. The bales teeter, barely contained by wires and wooden cribs, and dry grass swirls through the air, kept aloft for a time by the turbulence and speed of oil tankers and long-haul trucks and cars going by. I can imagine the last wisps of it floating over the coastal hills, the slopes and curves of which swirl and pool with countless kinds of glacial soils—muck and gravel and clay and loam, soils which the Algonquin with their wooden and stone tools had no choice but to follow and which the first colonists tried to remake in the image of the world they'd come from, the swirl that exists still, even now that prosperity has been parsed from cultivation.

The land where we live, monetarily, is worth more now than ever before, while the Grange as a political force has become as marginal as the hay crop. The National Grange had been organized in the second part of the nineteenth century with the intent of consolidating the power of farmers so as to counter an increasing exploitation by the railroads and middlemen. It had a social aim as well: against the urban world, the farming life was seen as backward, and the Grange founders hoped to help farm families beat back that growing perception. They were determined to shore up the place of the farmer, both to dignify it again—revitalizing Jefferson's dream of the cultivator of the earth as the ideal citizen—and to make the farmer fit to meet the modern world. *Attend to every duty promptly,* directs a nineteenth-century pamphlet, *and keep constantly before the minds of the members, the important fact that the great and grand object and the crowning glory of our organization is to "EDUCATE AND ELEVATE THE AMERICAN FARMER."* But it was no longer a farmer's world alone, and the place they maintained would always be self-conscious, would always exist in relation to another kind of life. I'll always remember that my father would wash up and change his clothes before going to the bank, and he would always take the car, not the truck, to do his business.

Though its political aims have long since faded, the rituals of the Grange, which were tied to the structure of the English manor house, remain intact. Officers continue to carry titles commensurate with that world: Overseer, Master, Steward, Assistant Steward . . . When there is a new inductee for membership, the Assistant Steward leads the blindfolded candidate around and around the hall floor, which stands in for an English field: *To reach the Master's office we must cross an enclosed field, which we enter by crossing this stile. [Leads the candidate over the steps.] This portion of the field is being drained. Before us is a deep ditch, across which is a narrow bridge. Step with care. [Leads the candidate over the bridge.] We now enter the woods where the Laborers are at work chopping, preparatory to clearing the field. [The sound of chopping is imitated by four of the officers clapping their hands with regularity.] We here come to a narrow path in which there are obstructions. Step slowly and with care. [Leads the candidate over the obstructions.] As we leave the woods we find before us a freshly plowed field, which we must cross. The ground is soft and mellow, step carefully. [Leads the candidate over plowed ground.] Once, twice, three* times, four turns around the hall, and with each turn a world comes more fully into order. First a new member is granted status as a Laborer, then Cultivator, Harvester, Husbandman. Or Maid, Shepherdess, Gleaner, Matron. There are now more women than men at the meetings. Daughters of farmers, widows of farmers.

"Your father was a member for years," Mrs. R—— said when she asked me to join the Grange in the months after his death. Her request reached the part of me that has always been uneasy with home, careful not to completely define myself as *here*. After all these years back, I am far more comfortable as an *I* in this place than as part of its *we*. It's an awkwardness that appears even when I sleep: I've dreamt of walking uphill in a dry field of waist-high hay. The way the field slopes uphill, I think it must be the one I used to pass as a child every weekday on the school bus, and every Sunday on the way to church. It would encompass my entire view for the moment we drove past: green in spring, flecked with insects and birds; the shadows and wind across the long grass in June, and again in late summer just before it was mowed a second time. Dried stubble. A field of snow. I think I was drawn to it even before I was aware it might be beautiful, the way it rose up toward the tall pines just beyond its crest where trees met sky. In my dream I hear it whispering as I wade through it. Then I come to a place where the field has been covered—tautly, neatly—with blankets and quilts. Some neighbors of mine appear and say they covered it because rain was coming and they wouldn't be able to get the harvest in before the storm. Their son, who used to take care of the haying, is no longer here, though I think he must still be everywhere in their world: even I think of him more often now that he has died, and always when I pass their house and the barn is wide open, and packed to the rafters with bales of hay. As I walk further up the field, I worry that I've made a mess of their blankets, which become more haphazard anyway, the more I dream, until the last parcel of the field is covered with bits of cloth of all kinds—calico and ticking, frayed corded bedspreads, rough canvas and old pillowcases . . .

I couldn't refuse Mrs. R——'s request to join, however awkward I felt, and I have been surprised by how comfortable I am when I occasionally attend Grange meetings and take my seat in a circle facing the others, my back to the stacks of folded tables along the north wall, or the jumbled goods along the south wall—toys and knickknacks, old baskets and racks of dresses and coats half covered with cloths and pushed into the corners to wait for the next yard sale. The expanse of maple floor between us shines with a half sheen: rich, old, worn into the present day. *Let the labors of the day begin,* the Gatekeeper announces. I touch my heart in greeting, and open my palm toward the center of the circle. Along with faith and charity, I pledge fidelity. I'm advised of the work of the season, just like everyone else: *Time to lift the mulch from your strawberries, time to put in the peas . . .*

When the piano starts up my voice strays a little behind the faithful as I sing "Simple Gifts" with a cluster of people who know almost nothing of my larger life but who knew me when I was young, and who've known my family always, whose quandaries are also my family's quandaries. It's a relief, a kind of simple seeing, far from my own ambitions and desires, since nothing is expected of me other than that my old child-self stand as representative of my family. What fidelity I have to the farm is taken for granted, a proper right, however much it can seem a mystery in the larger world.

Part of my ease, I know—and part of the assurance of the

place—has to do with the fact that everyone remembers my father in all the stages of his life, and they remember him to me often; it is through him that I'm included in the conversation after the formal part of the meeting breaks up, after everyone has set down their instruction manuals and laid aside their velvet sashes. The voices that had so stiffly recited the ceremony relax as we all become neighbors again, sitting down for coffee and cake, dwelling in the past. I hover at the table, a little awkward in the freer moments, without the ritual to give me my place. "Sit down, sit down—have some cake. How's your mother?" Mr. R——— will say to me. The stories start: "I remember it was the first time I ever saw electric lights, and I just kept turning the switches on and off, I couldn't believe it. Everyone thought I was simple . . ." Inevitably: "Your father, Christ, he was over eighty, and picking corn three times as fast as those boys . . ." Somewhere in the future may come a time when my memory of him will be confined to my own thoughts, but as long as the anecdotes are repeated and stories I've never heard continue to unfold, memory feels as if it is more white smoke than ash.

At the Grange, on those evenings, if you were to ask about the future, you would be met with a quietness, feel a privacy close in. There's not a farmer there who doesn't know, now that land prices have shot up, that the stone soil they've spent their lives plowing and planting, haying, weeding, has an untold worth, too much worth for more acreage to be devoted to farming. In farm families, when the last of the oldest generation dies, even if the land has been farmed for nearly four hundred years, when it is appraised for inheritance purposes it must be appraised for its "highest and best use," so it is di-

vided into theoretical house lots. The appraiser establishes
frontage distances and roadways, and imagines dwellings at
fixed intervals apart across back fields and lower fields. Since
it is often well drained and clear, farmland makes attractive
land for development. Lately in our town, prime one-acre
house lots along back roads have sold for more than
$150,000. The agricultural value placed on the same land
wouldn't be more than $3,000.

If no extraordinary provisions are made beforehand, such
an assessment often raises the value of a farm far beyond
what the inheritors will be able to pay in taxes. One of the
very few ways for the family to carry the farm through to another generation is to sell the development rights to the land.
This procedure constrains the future use of the land, restrict-
ing it to farming alone, and this restriction is written in the
deed so that every future owner of the land must abide by it.
No one ever discusses what will happen to the land when
there are no more farmers. With the worth of the land deval-
ued, much of the tax burden is lifted. Most families who
choose to follow such a route must make use of a combina-
tion of development rights bought by the state and bought by
the town to secure their land. They may have to go before a
town meeting to ask for public funds. Even in the most gener-
ous case, farmers won't receive the full development value of
the land, since the state and town cannot afford to pay them
what a developer would pay them. Such a course of action not
only opens up the private family world to the scrutiny and de-
bate of the public, it forecloses future choice. It can never do
justice to all a family's wishes—each child has his or her own
interest and ideas.

It's not surprising to me that few farmers avail themselves

of the option to sell their development rights: it goes against a grain deep in most of them, who have viewed the land itself as their only legacy, integral to their lives and to their sense of independence, which has always gone along with working the land. They cannot imagine it may be different after their time. *We live in a dream world,* writes the contemporary political commentator George Monbiot. *With a small, rational part of the brain, we recognise that our existence is governed by material realities, and that, as those realities change, so will our lives. But underlying this awareness is the deep semi-consciousness that absorbs the moment in which we live, then generalises it, projecting our future lives as repeated instances of the present. This, not the superficial world of our reason, is our true reality . . . The future has been laid out before us, but the deep eye with which we place ourselves on Earth will not see it.*

In wider conversations about land preservation, the idea of the farm can be swept up with the more general idea of saving "open space," which might include any land not yet built on—swamps and woods, brook beds. Sometimes the fields themselves have not for a long time been seen as private but rather, in the diminished state of farming, have become associated with the character of the town, with the idea of a place, and their visibility is deemed their most attractive asset. The public conversation often turns to talk, not of crops and what can be best grown on a given field, or the quality of the soil and the incline of the hills, but of "viewsheds"—the way the farm looks to those going by on the road. The workscape has become a landscape pulled out of reason and proportion by a community's desires and memories.

Our own farm lies on both sides of one of the main roads

into town, and the selectmen and town manager are eager to
have it preserved. "We have always been a farming town,"
they say, "and what better view to give those entering town
than real working fields." It will take a consensus of the wider
family to preserve it. The original farm of the 1901 deed is
owned by my father's remaining brothers. The newer fields
my father had acquired in his life are owned by my mother,
and the farm as a modern operation is viable only if all the
acreage and buildings on both properties are used in concert.
We were never prepared for this time—maybe no one ever is.
The farm we were raised on had at times seemed to be the
possession of all of the extended family. At other times it felt
to me as if it was possessed by my father and brother alone.
Sometimes I believe their quarreling was one of the ways the
farm remained theirs, that it kept the rest of us from true in-
volvement, kept anyone else from venturing a say. "I would
like to have tried it," my sister says about farming here, all
these years later, though she has built her own cleared place a
hundred miles away.

Even in the days just before my father died you could see
the boundaries they had set together. My father was in the
hospital by then, in and out of coherence. My brother was
late in coming. Where was he? When he finally walked
through the door, I saw how nothing in the world could have
touched the light across my father's face. I suppose if he had
any last things he wanted to say, he would have wanted to say
them to my brother. As it was, his unsteady voice was full of
wonder and gratitude: "You came."

I count ourselves lucky that Dave has stayed on through
the years and has kept the cultivation in a steady state. We
have had the luxury of time to consider what to do with the

farm, though we are all still unsure whether these days mark a beginning or an end, or remain an interim. Since no one in the family currently farms the land, the idea of its future feels diffuse, there's nothing specific to rally round, or to oppose. When my brothers and sister come back to visit, we have tentative discussions about how we might go about preserving the farm for the long future. We each have our own idea of what its future should be, just as we each have our own memories of it. To be responsible for so much land and yet to be separated from the work of the land itself is its own weight: the farm in our minds is growing more distant and abstracted. We are a loose confederation of siblings, no longer tied to place in fact, only in memory. We try to imagine what Dad would have done. We talk about what our mother might need for the future. How do you know what the future needs? It may be that the only way to preserve the farm would be to turn it into a kind of agrotourist destination with hayrides, apple picking, popcorn, petting zoos. Then it may no longer be understood as necessary to any kind of daily life, but may stand only as a symbol of necessity. Preservation, then, would be the most self-conscious of acts.

Sometimes I imagine this place will become a somewhere as clear and clean as the salt marshes. Removed from the human press of time, it will empty itself of memory, tracing itself back before our incursions on the land, and all the decisions, all the weight of human desires that were once imposed on it: the accumulation of judgments, the calculations, the care and the exploitations, attempts, histories, and abandonments. It will become close to an abstraction—"open space"—absent work, absent that exhaustion at dusk after a long day in the open air. Absent, too, will be the way a house feels when you come in from working in a storm, or in the cold, when the warmth rushes your face and makes you weak, tells you you don't need strength or endurance anymore—the relief of that—and the indoor quiet amid the bright domestic colors leaves you feeling a little deaf, even when you come in from the silence of a rimy October morning. "Open space" ready to be filled with a hundred dreaming gazes.

If it is open, at least it isn't abandoned or empty, the way places on the prairie now stand empty only a scant century after almost all the big bluestem was plowed under and planted in Old World grains and corn, after the frontier moved on and what was left behind came to be known as the heartland where you can trace by air the grid that laid out a world into great lots. *First it was a dirt road, narrow between two hedges, with a car crawling along it dragging a tail of dust,* noted a pilot flying over the Midwest. *Then the road turned off, but the line went straight ahead, now as a barbed wire fence through a large pasture, with a thin footpath trod out on each side by each neighbor as he went, week after week, year after year, to inspect his fence. Then the fence stopped, but now there was corn on one side of the line and something green on the other.*

Many midwestern counties are losing their population, and what rural jobs exist are not often agricultural: agriculture long ago married industry, and is now dependent on subsidies. It is a story that repeatedly appears in the *New York Times*: *Big farmers used their government checks to expand their acreage, buying small neighboring farms, and increased their production, which pushes down the world market price. They are still profitable, because government subsidies make up the difference . . . In Nebraska, nearly 70 percent of all farmers rely on government largesse to stay in business. Yet the biggest economic collapse is happening in counties most tied to agriculture—in spite of the subsidies.* Those bigger farms require more and larger machinery, which demands more production to make the enterprise profitable. There is a liability in the expanse of the land, in endless possibility. More production demands more acreage for farming, and farmers find themselves competing for whatever becomes available: *In the complicated equation that is modern agriculture, the mere size of one's farm can mean the difference between prosperity and failure. The competition to snap up whatever becomes available—the "land battle," one farmer here called it—can be fierce. Increasingly expensive tractors and combines and other mounting overhead costs . . . have led some farmers, whose families once planted just a few hundred acres, to farm as much land as possible . . . "You have to spread these costs over more acres . . . Every farmer feels the need to grow. That's just the way the business is."*

Meanwhile the grid has moved skyward: we are more familiar with images, not of men guiding self-scouring plows, but of men walking on steel beams seventy stories above street level, while the same story plays itself out again and again as populations all over the world leave the countryside for cities, making much the same sojourn as the New England farm girls had in the early nineteenth century, and as my grandparents had in later decades. Now there are almost twice as many people in New York City as there are on all the farms in America. *We are a cross-section of the entire world . . . a densely crowded ethnic hodgepodge, and the potential for chaos is enormous,* Paul Auster writes from the city. And: *We are the true heartland.* The word feels no more fitting for

New York City than it does for the Midwest in a country where human experience refuses to be fixed in place, where every place absorbs change and shifts beneath our feet, and in our imagination, country of eternal immigrants now with our inner resistances in tow, now with our inner resistances breached.

In the prayers of the Grange the afterlife is called *the Paradise not made with hands*. It is this I keep remembering long after I've forgotten our secret password and secret handshake, when to stand up, sit down, after the rest of the rote and ritual fall away. The phrase itself suggests both an allegiance to the love of the labor and the dream of release from the love of the labor. I wonder what this place will be without these farmers. What does it mean to want their life to remain, to count on them for a sense of gravity, even as I could never abide the same demands for myself? I keep thinking of this one evening when after cake and coffee we all go out into the night. The clocks have been turned back, it has been dark for hours, the air is dense as sable. My neighbors are hunched into their bulky coats and they call to each other—"Cold . . ." "Maybe rain . . ." "Good night . . ." " 'Night . . ."—as they walk toward their cars by ones and twos. It seems to me that the dark mythologizes them. I feel myself mythologize them, my own separate life mythologizes them. They remind me of Brueghel's drawing *The Beekeepers*, with its three methodical, slow-moving men clothed in protective frocks, isolated each to each. One is carrying a hive away, one is lifting the lid off another hive, the central figure is moving toward or away from a task. They aren't looking at one another or moving outside the work as they walk among their hives concentrating and alone. Their stout bodies are hardly animate, hardly even clay—when I first saw the drawing I thought it was unfinished, that the faces had not yet been drawn, and they reminded me of ancient, severely pruned apple trees with limbs cut off mid-twist, no longer reaching skyward in taut and graceful contortions, but querying forward, until slowly I understood it was really the beekeepers' gauze masks I was seeing, covering the stiff extended hoods of their robes. Their facelessness makes them appear a little furtive as they go about their tasks, though in truth they are no match for the heavy but agile boy—free of protective clothing—who, behind their backs, is sneaking up a tree, advancing toward a wild hive. *He who knows the nest knows it*, says the proverb in the lower left corner of the drawing. And *He who steals it has it.*

Yet even as I wonder about the old life of farming, a new, less obvious life is taking hold. There are always a few men and women, new to farming, who cultivate a handful of acres here and there, or come back to old places after having lived away. Their holdings may be no larger than the first few acres set atop the village at Patuxet, and they are sometimes dismissed as "hobby farmers." The markets they serve may seem rarified: goat cheese and antique apples, for instance. That they have established a new world of their own choosing may be a part of the dismissal: they can appear freer on the land, cultivating a past free from the past, without the confinements of a personal history. We always seem to want farmers to be flinty and difficult, born to it somehow. I caught myself at it when I learned that José Bové, the French activist farmer who'd dismantled a McDonald's and has served time in jail in his stand against agribusiness and genetically modified crops, had come to farming after years of being a college activist. I'd felt a little disappointed that his passion hadn't risen up out of the old life.

My neighbor who has come back to her family's place after a lifetime of teaching in other states, wanting to meet a little way the idea of a self-sufficiency, to raise a few chickens, hay, have a garden of her own, says, "We need to keep the land open, there might come a day when we'll need it again." Her words may at first seem fanciful, or wishful in their implication of necessity, but she is perilously correct. Massachusetts grows only 15 percent of its own food now, and however full and gleaming the supermarkets appear, there are only three days' supply of food on the grocery shelves. You need all kinds of men and women working the land to preserve agriculture, to do the work of feeding a thousand, or five, or one. Yes, you save a small patch of land, and the hope is that one here, one there, discontinuous as it may be, small as it may be, will somehow keep a ceiling lifted, and bring pressure to bear from below as the world moves on. It isn't inconceivable at all that we may need to fall back on ourselves and our labors, and the land underneath our feet, which carries the mistakes and knowledge of centuries, that we may need the land to mean once again what it had meant. *We heard a distant tapping on the road*, Edwin Muir wrote in his poem "The Horses," as he imagined recovery after catastrophe:

A deepening drumming; it stopped, went on again
And at the corner changed to hollow thunder.
We saw the heads
Like a wild wave charging and were afraid.
We had sold our horses in our fathers' time
To buy new tractors. Now they were strange to us

As fabulous steeds set on an ancient shield
Or illustrations in a book of knights.
We did not dare go near them. Yet they waited,
Stubborn and shy, as if they had been sent
By an old command to find our whereabouts
And that long-lost archaic companionship.
In the first moment we had never a thought
That they were creatures to be owned and used.
Among them were some half-a-dozen colts
Dropped in some wilderness of the broken world,
Yet new as if they had come from their own Eden.
Since then they have pulled our ploughs and borne our loads,
But that free servitude still can pierce our hearts.
Our life is changed; their coming our beginning.

The boundaries of our farm have stayed the same for as long as I've known them: what has been woods has remained woods; fields, fields. But as the world surrounding it has increased in density, as most other farms have gone out and the valley population has grown and spread into suburbs, the possibilities of the farm have grown. The small farmstand I worked in as a child had become a store by the time I returned—my brother saw to that—and now, along with what is grown on the farm, Dave sells milk, pies, bread, and juice. He travels to the Chelsea wholesale market to bring back lemons, limes, potatoes, and onions. He is blurring the line between here and there. His customers are busy people and would like to stop once for everything they need.

"It's something to see," Dave had said of the Chelsea Mar-

ket, and he asked me if I might like to go in one morning.
"Sure." We left well before sunup, maybe 4 a.m., though already the interstate into Boston was scattered with early driv-
ers heading for work, and more and more joined us as the
city skyline grew closer. It looked as it often does to me,
approaching it from the north—a kind of cartoon of a city
hugging the curve of the earth. You see the twentieth
century—the financial district, the Prudential, the Hancock—
long before you see the seventeenth, eighteenth, nineteenth
centuries: Beacon Hill, the State House, the Customs House
tower with its eagles of Cape Ann granite. Since it was summer the towns along the way were hidden behind maples,
oaks, and white pine, and the city seemed to rise out of green.
It appeared as if we were only an artery flowing toward sky-
scrapers.

We exited the highway before the descent into the city, just
as traffic was slowing a bit, and entered into flat country full
of rivers and creeks wending their way toward Boston Harbor. I could sense right away how it must once have been
marshland—the lay of the land was so low and level. On the
land beyond the warehousing and houses and industry, I knew
that phragmites would have taken hold. It's a taller, coarser
grass than salt hay—it's wild with height, as high as the big
bluestem of the old prairie: when you are in it, you can only
see straight up. In other places in the world phragmites had
been used for thatch and for paper. Here it is considered an
invasive species, a threat to the remaining salt marshes since it
grows voraciously in places where the flow of tides has been
restricted by development, where the salinity is lower. Phragmites proliferates by rhizomes, the way big bluestem once
had, and like bluestem comes back stronger if it is burned. Its

plumes of purple go gray in fruiting time. They say it's going to outlast everything.

In a small truck like Dave's you feel overwhelmed on the road to Chelsea long before you reach the market. You are swamped in a phalanx of long-haul trucks gearing down, trundling along the narrow streets among dark sleeping houses. All night long they've been hauling their goods against the flow of the old migrations, making noise like the sea at a distance, hauling their cargoes across international borders and state lines, through weigh stations and toll-booths, across bridges, through tunnels, carrying the world and all its seasons. The sound of their gears is heir to the whistle of the train Thoreau had heard from his cabin *sounding like the scream of a hawk sailing over some farmer's yard, informing me that many restless city merchants are arriving within the circle of the town, or adventurous country traders from the other side . . . Here come your groceries, country; your rations, countrymen! Nor is there any man so independent on his farm that he can say them nay. And here's your pay for them! screams the countryman's whistle . . . I watch the passage of the morning cars with the same feeling that I do the rising of the sun, which is hardly more regular. Their train of clouds stretching far behind and rising higher and higher, going to heaven while the cars are going to Boston . . . There is no stopping to read the riot act, no firing over the heads of the mob, in this case. We have constructed a fate, an Atropos, that never turns aside. (Let that be the name of your engine.)*

Once we were among the market buildings—long, low warehouses that could just as well have been housing air conditioners, washing machines, or latex paint—I could see men built like stevedores zip pallets stacked with crates across the cement floors. I could hear voices amid the bleating of the backup warnings. "Got to move product." Everything seemed to be called "product": clementines, frost-sensitive avocados, winter-hardy cabbages, Chinese eggplant and Italian eggplant, tomatoes sized and sorted and priced for every market: grape and cherry, greenhouse slicers grown in a soilless mix, field-ripened from the southern hemisphere, tomatoes still on their vines, wrapped in paper, or wrapped in plastic. There's little reason anymore to be bound by soil or climate, latitudes and ocean currents, or the till the ice ages left behind. Everyone can have peaches, rhubarb, and strawberries in midwinter, though the price and frequency and quality still depend on soils somewhere, and on sun and rain. On any given day in the Chelsea Market the pineapples may be at their peak and smell sweet, but the melons may still be green, the grapefruit of fair quality, and the quantity of plums insufficient to quote. The air never clears of the myriad scents of the tropic and the northern, all latitudes, every scent converging along with every season. Most food now travels more than 1,300 miles before it settles on someone's dinner plate—20 percent of the traffic on the roads serves the food system—and before it settles on a plate it must converge in a terminal market like Chelsea where the same varieties of apples may be offered from China, Washington State, New York, and maybe even New Hampshire, and they will be far more uniform than the ones Thoreau found on his walks more than a hundred and fifty years ago: *In 1836 there were in the garden of the London Horticultural Society more than fourteen hundred distinct sorts. But here are species which they have not . . . There is, first of all, the Wood Apple (*Malus sylvatica*); the Blue-Jay*

Apple; the Apple which grows in Dells in the Woods
(sylvestrivallis), also in Hollows in Pastures (campestrivallis);
the Apple that grows in an old Cellar-Hole (Malus cellaris);
the Meadow Apple; the Partridge Apple; the Truant's Apple
(cessatoris), which no boy will ever go by without knocking
off some, however late it may be; the Saunterer's Apple,—you
must lose yourself before you can find the way to that; the
Beauty of the Air (decus aëris); December-Eating; the Frozen-
Thawed (gelato-soluta), good only in that state . . .

I believed the entire world was converging there on that
built-up marsh, and would be bartered for, and then dispersed
to other corners of the earth. Amid the noise, the rush, the
large trucks, the pallets stacked high with crates, I felt how
small our own enterprise was, and how defensive was my feeling for it. I wanted to believe the smaller world would persist
as something more than a last illusion, as a stay against the
confusion, and I thought I could see neighborhood shopkeep-
ers going from merchant to merchant each on their own worn
path—the same as a deer through a woods—to favored vendors. The Chinese proprietors sought out their own, and
would carry lemongrass and Asian greens back to their neighborhoods; the Italians, eggplant and peppers and squash; the
Hispanics, yucca, calabaza, sugarcane.

As we walked through, Dave talked mildly about buying
in some early corn: "Everybody is already asking for it." It
would be another month before his own would be ripe, but
the stores had long been stocked with sugar-enhanced and su-
persweet varieties—sweeter than the local ever had been. For
decades there had never been a crop more tied to locale than
corn, available in our part of the world from mid-July to the
frost. It had evolved from Indian meal to sweet corn, and

sweetness had become its most fleeting, desired characteristic: its sugars turned to starch the minute it was picked from the stalk. Sayings grew up around it. "You've got to have the water boiling before you pick it." "It's no good the second day." Local farmstands depended on that urgency, they were the only ones who could assure a daily freshness, but in the last several decades science has enabled sweetness to keep, a sweetness that swamps the old cornier and mild sweetness, that can make corn taste like candy, really, even days after it's been picked and shipped. In doing so it has removed some of the allure from the local.

Long since those eight sketched fields of it shown on Samuel de Champlain's map of Port St. Louis, corn has become the predominant crop on American soil. It now has more uses than the Wampanoag could have dreamed with their steamed cakes and parched maize in their hunting pouches. We don't even think about most of the corn we consume. High-fructose corn syrup—so much cheaper than sugar—flavors sodas and sweets, and the cattle who once thrived on a diet of salt hay, and then tame grasses, now live on a diet of corn, which enables beef cattle to gain weight more quickly and to be raised year-round. The beef is marbled and fatty, which is what we have come to prefer even though corn plays havoc with their health, making antibiotics a necessity.

Feedlots have shrunk the need for large areas of pasture and hay, and the herds are concentrated down into a muddy, trampled pen where cattle stand in piles of their own manure, and in the hot dry evenings plumes of manure dust travel on the wind. Lagoons of manure leak and sometimes burst, or send ammonia and methane into the air. Zinc and copper, which had been added to the feed, build up in soils because of the overapplication of manure onto cropland. In her book on new infectious diseases, *Secret Agents*, Madeline Drexler writes: *The site of modern meat production is akin to a walled medieval city, where waste is tossed out the window, sewage runs down the street, and feed and drinking water are routinely contaminated by fecal material. Each day, a feedlot steer deposits 50 pounds of manure, as the animals crowd atop dark mountains composed of their own feces.*

What does a field mean now, a field that had its beginning in the vast expansions of those first colonial settlements into space for their cattle, the dream of the English field, its order and correctness and idea of husbandry, the space that spurred the war with Philip, that distinguished a world from the wild, that spread even to the salt marshes? As the early planes take off from Logan and the sun rises over Deer Island, over the bones of Christian Indians who died there during the winter of Philip's War, the produce prices in the market are dropping amid the smells of concrete, waxed cardboard, plastic, diesel, of vegetable rot and of ripeness: cold keeps the produce fresh only for so long—once it is on the open market, it begins to spoil, and tomorrow more will be coming from Florida, Mexico, Australia, New Zealand, and California. They say "the produce starts in California and comes across the country. After Boston, there's only Boston Harbor." The Haymarket vendors are moving in to take advantage of the morning surplus, and representatives from the food banks scour the place for donations. Somewhere beyond us the phragmites stirs in the first breezes of the morning.

6

WILDERNESS

In recent years a few of the local farmers, those who've been determined to continue, have sold their family holdings in the area and moved north to Vermont, New Hampshire, or Maine, following the old migrations up the rivers, inching toward the limits of wide cultivation, adapting to different soils, to colder valleys with shorter growing seasons, nearer the steeper lands that, before white settlement, had been largely the province of hunter-gatherer tribes. The sale of their old farms buys two, three times the acreage in the north and also, strangely enough, places them in a stronger farming community—or at least in a less suburban one, where many yards still contain vegetable gardens fenced off from deer. Though the move may appear to be sudden—after the death of a child, say—always I think the decision must have been long in coming. Often it leaves rumor whispering behind—"How much did you say he sold the land for?"—that persists even after the old fields and orchards have filled in with horseshoe streets, and other dreams have taken hold. For myself, I still think of the north as its own country, one that takes me out of the world I know, and I go there when I simply need to walk clear of it all.

It's said New Hampshire's White Mountains were named by sailors who saw the distant winter peaks from their ships, elemental and inhospitable as the gray-green Atlantic they were sailing on. By now all the summits of those ranges have been climbed, blazed, recorded, and owned, written about, legislated, and regulated, though to me they can feel as if they're still purely imagined, the way they were before maps, before trails cut through them. The name, anyway, is as true now as then: white, meaning fully luminous, the color of salt and milk, of frantic seas and the albatross. Even on a clear, warm June day when they are gray-blue rock against a summer sky, the summits of the Franconia Range—Lafayette, Lincoln, Little Haystack—seem nearly inaccessible and beyond human bearing—as far as a sailor's glimpse of them. *Those sublimer towers*, Melville called them, *whence, in peculiar moods, comes that gigantic ghostliness over the soul at the bare mention of that name . . .*

Thoreau knew what it meant to climb such peaks. Maine's Mount Katahdin caused him to write: *Some part of the beholder, even some vital part, seems to escape through the loose grating of his ribs as he ascends. He is more lone than you can imagine. There is less of substantial thought and fair understanding in him, than in the plains where men inhabit. His reason is dispersed and shadowy, more thin and subtile like the air. Vast, Titanic, inhuman Nature has got him at disadvantage, caught him alone, and pilfers him of some of his divine faculty. She does not smile on him as in the plains. She seems to say sternly, why came ye here before your time? This*

ground is not prepared for you. Is it not enough that I smile
in the valleys? I have never made this soil for thy feet, this air
for thy breathing, these rocks for thy neighbors. I cannot pity
or fondle thee here, but forever relentlessly drive thee hence to
where I am kind.

As I stand at the trailhead at the base of Mount Lafayette
on this June day I do feel free and clear, but also a little overwhelmed at the thought of the climb—elevation 5,260 feet—
for the top really does look like another country, and the
clusters of hikers I see picking their way across an exposed
ridge look like burdened pilgrims heading for another life. But
the trail in front of me, an old bridle path, is wide and obvious from nearly two hundred years of use. As early as the
1820s large hiking parties ascended Lafayette—first known as
the Great Haystack—on foot and horseback: rusticators, ad-
venturers, tourists, and botanists who'd gained the trailhead
by way of wagon, then steam rail. They climbed through the
industrial revolution—dressed in dun-colored woolens and
leather boots—and a handful of wars; they slept in the grand
hotels in the Notch and took their ease at the top in a stone
summit house; they climbed through the haze of timberland
fires burning on the flanks of the mountains, then through the
atomic age, and the age of information, until it is our own
strange selves walking in their footsteps, arrayed as we are in
reflective and fluorescent microfibers, big in the shoulders,
never out of reach of voices, looking like bright daubs of
paint against the subtle colors of the landscape. So many have
ascended that experienced hikers sometimes derisively call this
path the "Bridle Trough."

Even in its well-worn state it feels entirely challenging to
me. As a child I'd wandered freely through our mild, cut-over

woods around the farm, but I'd climbed only a few modest peaks when I was young, and since I'd been part of a larger group—from school, say, or 4-H camp—I was always insulated from the larger challenges of the trail. Now I'm always cautious when I climb on my own, but I like the alertness it takes, the way the need to feel a bit apprehensive also makes you feel a bit new, the way I do now as I face the trail, which begins by rising up on gradual switchbacks sheltered in the dappled light of birches. It's easy going for the first mile, on a path of moss and soft dirt that is still tied to a kind of valley-world forest with its familiar, moist smells of duff and acid earth. Then a set of stone steps carries me toward the ridge, and the birches drop away. The trail narrows and steepens as it begins its climb through straight, true red spruce and hemlock. I get the first hint of the tonic scent I have been waiting for: spicy, sharp, northern, the scent of a world that cannot possibly be cultivated. Where red spruce grows, the frost-free days are too brief, and the growing season too short to be of much use for farming. The woods become less and less characteristic as I go. Soon the spruce begins to grow stunted, no taller than human height, and toughened by the cold and exposure of the higher elevation. The ridgeline trail narrows, the smells grow even sharper and less intimate, the soil on the path is gone. It's no longer a thoughtless ascent as I clamber over rocks and work up narrow chutes of tumbled stone, and sometimes rely on the staunch trail-side trees to pull myself up. Some have been grabbed by so many hands that their bark is polished smooth.

On every side of me the season is retreating: flowers that had already bloomed and shriveled in the birch woods are in full bloom among the spruce: drooping yellow heads of the bluebead lilies nod toward the earth, and the bunchberries are a creamy whorl of petals. I grow cold when I stop for more than a minute. Further on, the bluebeads and bunchberries are still buds, and red spruce gives way to balsam and black spruce, which in turn grow lower and lower—shoulder height, then waist height, growing as they can, sculpted and half killed by wind, rime, ice, and snow. It's not that they were made for the place, it's that little else can survive. Tight, uncountable growth rings mark incremental yearly progressions. They may be older than any trees that tower over the valley trail, maybe they'd been old even back in the heyday of the grand hotels in the Notch, when the logging railroads followed the East Branch of the Pemigewasset River into the prime forests. Now two young girls, their backpacks sagging under the weight of hats and windbreakers, chocolate, water, and raisins, pause among a ragged clump of them. The ridge drops off steeply from where they are gazing out at the fir-covered, rock-scarred slope of Mount Lincoln. I hear one, in a clear, pure voice, exclaim: "Don't you just want to fly? Don't you wish you were a bird?"

If you climb high enough, you enter a world with its own vocabulary, one specific to geologists and climbers: boreal, alpine, strange. Two hours from the valley floor, the shallow intractable eye of a nearby bog is called a *tarn*. And *col*, meaning neck, little saddleback, is a dip in the ascent, a sheltered respite where wood sorrel spangles the duff. What trees there are lie nearly prostrate, no more than knee high, with sparse flecks of green among mostly bare and bleached tops the color of driftwood, great rags of it, flagging stiffly away from the prevailing winds. It's called *krummholz*, and everything weak about it has been pruned away by scouring, steady gales and winter ice that beards the branches. Thoreau, when he climbed Mount Katahdin, walked on top of such trees, and they supported his full weight. On a perfectly clear June day, the sun strong, the warblers darting in and out of cover, krummholz alone makes the harshness of the place fathomable.

Several trails converge near the col, and there is a wooden shelter where hikers can get fresh water, splash the salt off their faces, and sleep overnight in summer. Benches, wood floors, pine tables, cookstove, much of it was hiked in more than half a century ago. In early afternoon the caretaker stands in the long cool shadows of the kitchen punching down bread dough and shaping long loaves for a second rise. An old man just down from the summit rinses out his shirt and hangs it over a railing to dry. On summer nights the hut comes to life at the end of the day as hikers who'd arrived in ones, twos, fours, sevens congregate for a noisy and jovial dinner. Afterward there's chatting, and games among children. Some walk off to see the sun go down over the western mountains, the moon come up in the east. The night distorts the distances so that the ridges ahead—the way to go—seem unfathomable, and the lit town to the northeast feels as far off as the summer stars. In that remoteness you can feel strange among so many people, maybe a little resentful that so many have come the same way. You might want a clear quiet.

On a night I spent there years ago I lay in bed after the lights were put out and imagined how we all disappeared to that world, to the million stars, to the dark humps of scarred and toughened land. Were we dreaming of becoming kin to the people Crèvecœur had imagined after agriculture—*a still simpler people divested of every thing beside hope, food, and raiment of the woods: abandoning the large framed house, to dwell under the wigwham?* I tossed fitfully in my bunk in a room where twenty others slept, each one curled under three gray wool blankets. In the night someone opened the door for air, a little later someone else closed it against the cold. Below us: stunted spruce running down into the valley; above, the soilless, exposed world beyond treeline. And we slept, souls on the edge of *something*. Someone talked on and on in his sleep, another sighed and turned toward the wooden wall. Snores deep and grainy, snores light and aspiring, puffs of breath, simple even breathing, stops and starts, and—once in a while—startling gaps of no breath at all made a kind of night music of the exhausted.

Past the hut and the col, the spruce—even in its wind-stunted state—soon disappears entirely, and I lift myself above treeline where cairns mark the way over rocks and boulders and tumbled stones. Beyond agriculture, and then beyond timber, there is nothing to do but put one foot in front of the other and look out on the vast stretches of earth, at the patches of grasses and alpine flowers pushed to this extreme by the advance of the spruce forest when the last of the ice melted away. Here they can thrive without competition, as they once thrived in the ice ages, and do now in the Arctic, small and hunkered to bear the winds, the cold, the short growing season. Meadow grasses, and flowers, worts, mosses. Lichen on everything, on the last of the blown twigs, on rocks and scoured earth. On such land Thoreau sounded as bewildered as a spaceman tumbling out beyond Pluto: *This was that Earth of which we have heard, made out of Chaos and Old Night. Here was no man's garden, but the unhandselled globe*

. . . What is it to be admitted to a museum, to see a myriad of particular things, compared with being shown some star's surface, some hard matter in its home! I stand in awe of my body, this matter to which I am bound has become so strange to me. I fear not spirits, ghosts, of which I am one,—that my body might,—but I fear bodies, I tremble to meet them. What is this Titan that has possession of me? Talk of mysteries! Think of our life in nature,—daily to be shown matter, to come in contact with it,—rocks, trees, wind on our cheeks! the solid *earth!* the actual *world!* the common sense! Contact! Contact! Who *are we?* where *are we?*

How different it must have been for him, who had to cut his own way up the mountain, who'd climbed above treeline out of an agrarian society in a time when the quality of soil marked your life and determined your chances, when almost everyone lived according to the seasons, and a summit was the limit of the extreme, yet attainable, world, back before speed and flight, and the modern city rising up in glass and steel, before small talk and golf on the moon, and the photograph of our solitary blue planet, floating within the permutations of its clouds in the black *no* of space.

To ascend still feels rare to me, especially in the last moments of the climb, when I am hunched down, clambering over the strewn stones, placing every foot and hand, reading the hard surfaces from cairn to cairn until I lift myself up to the highest point, and am at last free and upright and seeing everything of a vast, ever-flowing green world, all the living, and fallen, and decaying merged in a trackless expanse of green and green and green as my labored breath and heart slow and settle bit by bit in the absolved, exhausted ease of attainment. The top of Mount Lafayette is as high as I have ever climbed on earth.

Even here dozens are with me, milling around, resting, drinking, eating. I'm sure many have been higher—for some this is an almost usual day, for others this is a singular aspiration, and together we form a mountaintop society. Whispers and murmurs, talk rising and falling. "Do you have some water?" "Sure is beautiful." "Are you getting cold?" "We should get going before we stiffen up." A young girl applying moleskin to her heel reminds me of the alabaster statue in Rome of a boy pulling a thorn from his foot. Someone is crouched in the last remnants of the old summit house—all but the stone foundation has blown away—her face toward the sun. For now it *is* kind on the summit, the wind softly, pleasantly, buffets my ears, and nothing, no trees or edifices of any kind, stops it above me. To the west, and tiny, tiny down below, are the highway through the gap, the Cannon tram, white spires, clock towers, white clapboards on white trim, white, white, the settlers thought best to stand for order in the wilderness. Valley people contented with the valleys. My father never climbed a mountain so far as I know, nor my mother either.

Almost as striking as the vast views is the path that links summit to summit along the Franconia Range—just scrabble, the gravel of old ice ages—defined by a low scree wall: Lafayette slung to Lincoln, Lincoln to Little Haystack, Little Haystack to the peak beyond. If you follow it south you will reach Georgia, if you follow it north you'll reach Thoreau's Katahdin. The way to go on the ridge has been made as narrow—and full of possibility—as a walk beneath the barrel vaults of a monastery. The reason for the path is practical: we are too many to wander freely. Inheritors and intensifiers of the rusticators' dreams, we walk in such numbers one after another that a litany of alpine flowers have disappeared from the popular peaks. DO NOT STRAY FROM THE PATH, the signs have been saying along the way. CARRY OUT WHAT YOU CARRY IN. NO CAMPING. NO FIRES. NO SLEEPING ABOVE TREELINE.

All the footfalls have taken away some of the apprehension of the wild, since they largely free you from maps and compasses and the need to scale old snags to gain a long view. They've dissipated, too, the intense concentration and keenness that comes with relying on yourself to keep your place at all times, conscious of every footfall, and of what might be coming toward you: *Though in many of its aspects this visible world seems formed in love, the invisible spheres were formed in fright.* In good weather even a path the width of a harrow line through dense stands and flagrant undergrowth, one kept clear by only casual passings, one that might be lost in dark or rain or snow, is an ancestral trace not so distant from the arrow in the bone and the light of cooking fires. Then you can fully believe you only need keep clear what has been made, and go on. But in the instance of a cloudburst racing across from the west, you suddenly understand that the ease is all chance. We walk in danger of sudden storms, and fronts moving in, fog and cold and rain, and voices veering away like birds caught on a wind.

The eastward view from the top of Lafayette has no villages in it, no spires or white paint, just mountains beyond the mountains until they meet the soft and hazy far sky. This is the Pemigewasset Wilderness, the heart of the White Mountain National Forest, officially designated and protected. You are not gazing all the way back before design and ambition. It is only distance, the overview, that makes it appear as some kind of primordial beauty. All that unbroken forest has been inextricably mixed up with history, a part of our own complicated past, with its exploitations, its ideas of the romantic and

the sublime. Had I stood in my place among the ageless lichen
a century ago, I'd have seen huge clear-cuts where stands of
trees had been felled, trimmed, and dragged out. The cuts,
some reaching up the side of Mount Lafayette, would have
been littered with slash and deadfall. The East Branch and
Lincoln Railroad stretched into the timberlands by following the Pemigewasset River, and there were logging camps
throughout, painted red, and built so they could be taken
down and transported by train to be set up again farther in,
near new cutting operations along Cedar Brook, along the
flank of Mount Guyot, at North Fork junction . . .

   It took far less than a century to clear those tracts of land,
and for a while it was a world entirely its own. French-
Canadian loggers, Nova Scotians, and New Englanders lived
the winter in the woods, sawing and striking, felling tree after
tree. On a winter day snow squalls could obscure the entire
Franconia Range, and still they worked on, not seeing beyond
the world of their saws and chains, and the surrounding
snow-draped trunks of spruce. Some were trying to make
money for the sake of a little farm in kinder country, others
looked forward to a marriage, or worked to send money back
home. For some this was all, a life made of following the
work. And in the hours that weren't work, in the long northern night, a hundred men slept two to a bunk, snoring, spit-
ting on the floor, singing French songs in their sleep. Frost on
the windows as they slept on in the cold. Meat and dough-
nuts, brown bread and beans, salt cod on Fridays. Sundays
one of the men, sitting in a rocker cut from a barrel, might
read a paper to the others. Someone in a corner might whittle
an ax helve. Emerging from the woods to return to their farms
at sap season must have been like emerging from a fogbound

sea to realize they'd lived a parallel life, completely separate from village and farm. Remote, isolate, partial.

It is desperately clean work that is going on in the East Branch Wilderness. There was little talk—simply concentrated effort and energy, and throughout it all a perfectly apparent genius of direction, wrote one visitor to the logging camps. For however particular their individual dreams were, their collective efforts cleared the valleys, cleared half the east flank of Lafayette, and other peaks on the Franconia Range. Slash lay in great black heaps on the snow, then was covered by new snow, then shone with meltwater. It dried in the sere exposed heat of summer until a spark from the railroad lighted on the refuse, or lightning struck, say, on the east side of Owl's Head, as it did in August 1907, and the ensuing fire swept Mount Bond and burned over the easterly slope of Mount Garfield, the slope of Mount Guyot, and the northeasterly flank of Mount Lafayette.

The smoke, driven before the northwest wind, obscured farther mountains. It went beyond Lake Winnipesaukee and lay over the valleys to the ocean. Another current carried a long streak of smoke toward Vermont. The glow reflected on the clouds and caught the attention of summer visitors watching from their porches, for tourism was on the rise on the west flank of the range even as the timber prospects on the east side were playing out. Though large parties of men worked at fighting the fire, only rain and the dying of the winds ended it. A country, then, of charred stumps and dried stream beds. Though there had long been tensions between the logging and tourist industries in the mountains, when the smoke cleared it was obvious that tourism and logging could not coexist on the Franconia Range, at least not on the scale desired by both industries.

Now in the Pemigewasset Wilderness, the railroad bridges have dropped into abysses. The main hiking trail into those woods is the old railbed that follows the East Branch of the Pemigewasset. You slip onto it off a major highway, and walk on and around the last of the decaying wooden sleepers. Iron spikes shine out of the trail dust and softening wood. The old logging camps along the way have been burned to keep hikers from sleeping in them, or have been salvaged—some say you can still spot the distinctive red boards in the nearby towns— or have collapsed. But there are stone foundations here and there, and mossy, lichen-covered bridge abutments. The river that runs alongside has its source on the flank of Mount Lafayette. Its bed is of tumbled stone and boulders, and when the spring meltwater subsides, there are places shallow enough to cross on the rocks, and pools deep enough to swim in. I don't know why, but even five minutes in that water will leave your old skin feeling softer than a child's.

Almost in answer to all the ambition and excess determination of the timber barons comes an ambition and determination not only to obliterate the marks of those logging days but to create something absolutely pristine. The Wilderness Act of 1964 decrees that the land it protects shall be *an area where the earth and its community of life are untrammeled by man, where man himself is a visitor who does not remain . . . retaining its primeval character and influence, without permanent improvements or human habitations, which is protected and managed so as to preserve its natural conditions . . .* One of the insistences of a designated wilderness area is that no preexisting human structures are to be maintained, that the past should be encouraged to disappear. They say if you walk far enough into the Pemigewasset Wilderness you'll see the last railroad trestle still standing. I imagine it shrouded in woods and silence, the rock-strewn river running under it: care and time and effort abandoned just as in my own valley world. It stands odd, harmless, representative, and argued about vehemently. Some insist it is a nonconforming artificial structure in the wilderness that must be removed; others, an important historical artifact that by law must be preserved, suggesting everything of the long quarrel between remembrance and forgetting, of how much more than the swirl of snow, or the smoke and heat of fire, or the rate of decay separates us from the loggers who once worked there. It can seem that more than a century separates us. We hikers are now so many that we constitute our own genius of direction as the known world and the felt world, the maps of science and the maps of belief, become more distinct from one another.

And now the desire is not only to forget but to feel new in the wilderness. The extreme is considered more and more to be a testing place, matching the will against elevation, stone, and cold to make a hurt that keeps you from absence. The paths are not only maintained but made difficult. The Appalachian Trail has departed the valleys and towns and roadways—where habitation and wilderness might mingle—and has become more a trail of mountain ridges, full of desolate challenges. If you want to complete the Appalachian Trail today you'll have to wade through rough waters and crawl through icy caves. At the end of his journey, Earl Shaffer, a seventy-nine-year-old hiker who, in 1998, walked the trail for the third time in his life, couldn't disguise his bitter disappointment at the way the route had changed over time: *In 1965 the trail was perfect*, he said, *but they were not satisfied. They make all these changes. They seem to be obsessed with the idea that you have to make it as rough as possible . . . It's*

*an almost impossible trip. Who wants to go out and wade
across a 100-foot icy river barefoot?*

Who *are we?* where *are we?* Thoreau had asked, and it
seems to me the extreme did not define him. It undefined him.

When it's time to climb down I do so in a blur of weariness,
picking my way over the tumbled rocks on the path. I have to
hold myself back all the five miles and favor my left knee.
Halfway down I start to hear the trucks passing through the
notch on the highway. As the air grows more dense and the
trees regain their stately forms, I find myself half dreaming of
the summit still, and also half desiring home. The trail grows
softer underfoot as soil begins again to pad the trail. Everything is humming, including my nerve endings, and hums still
as I drive down the highway through the gap and into the
foothills where the Pemigewasset River flows into the higher
lakes of the region, where you can hear the loons calling off
the lakes—a call out of a time older than almost any other living thing. Loons thrived in prehistoric times, and they once
thrived in the kinder valley worlds to the south, though
they've been driven north by loss of habitat where their call
sounds rare and arresting: yodels, tremolos, wails, hoots, and
laughter at all hours across the water. They can set the coyotes
howling. Even when they are coaxed back to more southerly
waters, they don't return to the smaller ponds, which are
crowded now with camps and homes. They return to the
man-made Quabbin Reservoir, and call their weird calls over
the drowned towns there.

Soon after the water leaves the north lakes it becomes the
Merrimack River, and once I glimpse it—the interstate crosses
and recrosses the Merrimack—I begin to feel I am burning

back into my own atmosphere, happily tired, past ripening strawberry fields and peas with their laden pods hanging heavy on the trellised vines. I can see greenhouses with their sides peeled back and pink tomatoes within. The first mowing cut and baled across the fields. The water that is so soft to the skin in the East Branch is unenterable less than a hundred miles further south, having been severely compromised by fertilizers, pesticides, and salts coming off fields and parking lots and neighborhoods and businesses. The metals and dyes of closed factories are still buried in its mud. I see the river slowed and widened, shining in the last sun of the day. It cannot support salmon, nor can the little rivers running into it. Now in the valleys of the Merrimack and its tributaries, frequently the town hall doors—hundreds of years old, some of them, the green paint peeling—the doors we all walk through to pay taxes or to purchase hunting licenses or building permits, to register to vote, to look up the wetlands maps and zoning maps—have warnings tacked to them concerning the Beaver Brooks and Black Brooks, the Long Ponds and Silver Lakes that find their way into the Merrimack. A fish in a red circle with a slash through it: PREGNANT WOMEN AND CHILDREN SHOULD NOT EAT FISH TAKEN FROM THE FOLLOWING LAKES AND STREAMS . . . And still porch lights go on one by one. The color of the pines approaches their shadows, the blue sky deepens into dusk, and the sun sets in a red blaze behind a stand of trees, the color glinting off the side of a white barn, and then the peak of the barn.

Everything calls me back in the long June evening, and yet I can't get used to not seeing the shapes of the mountains. By the time I arrive home it's nearly dark, and I stand at my back door, holding open the screen, gazing, believing it should be enough to take in the orchard and its first fruits, and the white pines beyond. It's almost always been enough these last years, and calming in and of itself, this world that *is* characteristic. But tonight I feel there should be more behind the immeasurable night woods, some steep, rising, and challenging land. I keep listening for silence, keep desiring more, the *more* that makes unstable my allegiance to all I know. I keep imagining the wind-stunted red spruce, keep seeing them in dreams, seeing them for days wherever I look—and the ridge, the long walk in front of me on top of the world, the gaps, rock slides, and screes, the near trees ragged and ravaged by the elements, and beyond, as far as I can see, the vast blue assuaging Pemigewasset Wilderness.

7

GHOST COUNTRIES

There are times when, as night approaches, I sit on the stone step at the back of my house and watch the contours of the land grow more severe in the coming dark: the orchard hillside steepens as the swale disappears into the depths, and the pines tower in their shadows as if they were rising up to an older stature. After a while I can't tell where the tended acres end and the woods begin, and it feels as if the wild is crowding the farm back to the size of the first settlers' places, back before cattle arrived in this country, before tame grasses were cultivated and wide expanses were enclosed, when to every person was given only one acre of land. Later, when I lie down to sleep, I can imagine an unseen world emerging from the pines: foxes hunting among the apple trees, deer rooting out old squash and nosing the soil in the freshly turned beds. I sometimes hear the coyotes' erratic baying over their kill, or the owls calling to one another— softly at first, with each hoot distinct, then the calls quicken as they strengthen, growing closer and closer together until they overlap to make their concerted music. *The death of my father left me sad and depressed for a couple of months,* wrote Thomas Merton in the time before he began to search out his belief. *But that eventually wore away. And when it did, I found myself completely stripped of everything that impeded the movement of my own will to do as it pleased.* What is it that makes the wild feel so close? The foxes? The owls, calling from the bare boughs? Is it the deaths of so many that seem to have come so quickly, or the few who remain and are all that impede the movement of my own will?

After so many deaths and decisions leave you feeling light on the land, something has to move in. These subsided years on the farm are the time in which I've come to know my mother best. Our talk over meals isn't deflected by details about the farm or the work of settling my father's estate. Time isn't fraught with trips to the lawyers and the large decisions about what needs to be done. The conversations usually involve family, what everyone is doing, plans for visits, the holidays. My brother, who for so long ran the farm along with my father, is out west now, in Arizona, doing some carpentry, a little farming for people on the side, taking care of an old apple orchard that a retired couple took ownership of, helping with a vineyard, planting a garden. When we mention him the conversation is mild and incidental.

It's late for many things, and largely our relationship occupies present moments. I laugh a little now at myself, and the idea I had for my mother after my father's death—one I now see I devised for myself. I had imagined independence for her, that she would manage her own finances, travel some, at least take small trips throughout New England. Perhaps I wanted not just to ease my own day-to-day life but to ease some future memory of her. If she were in the world, going to the Grange, involved in the community, there would be a larger repository for memory: all the talk, talk, talk in a room like the Grange Hall where stories could grow in time.

My mother has always been quiet and inward, and she is even more so now that she is growing forgetful, but she is dreamy these days, too. It's as if she is freeing herself from almost everything, though she still remembers my father in a militant way, and she will never willingly leave "the house your father built for me." Yet as she has it, it is growing in over him. The exterior appears largely the same, modestly set back on its green lawn, but the place that accommodated us all easily is impractical for her alone, and now seems like a chambered shell. The rooms above her are clean and empty, and she lives in the center of the first floor amid a clutter of papers, of work she means to do, things she means to read, her lists, the TV on loud, her excitable dog by her side. She lets everything impractical reign. I aim to give in to it, saying to myself there is a great freedom in letting everything be, but when I enter I have to resist turning down her TV and putting up the shades during the day so as to make it more like the place I once knew.

I imagine when her memory goes a whole unknown world will disappear; she is the last in her own family's generation with any kind of memory: her parents are gone, and her two older sisters are well into their eighties, and remember little. When the three of them are together my mother is by far the most talkative. Most of the time among them is occupied with a contented silence, with their gazing out at the world. "They were always so close," she says of her sisters, the Irish twins— just eleven months apart. "I was so much younger, they just left me behind. And now . . ." Now one Irish twin will certainly recognize the other. We ask: "Do you know who this is?" "Yes, yes . . . my sister . . ." But between them, they barely patch together a coherent past, and both are forgetting my father. "Who did our sister marry?" they might ask each other. "What was his name?"

A highway runs through the first place they lived in the city of Lawrence, and urban renewal has razed the last. Almost all the stores they shopped at are gone—a few bakeries remain, a few markets tucked back in the side streets. You rarely hear Italian. For all the ambitions of the industrialists, that world did not endure as long as the world of the first white settlers had, or the world of the Algonquin before them. The jobs hardly lasted out my grandfather's working life, and little more than a hundred years after Lawrence was founded, the textile jobs moved south for the cheaper labor. Then the jobs that had gone south moved overseas, and the testimony of young Asian women who came out of their villages to work in the factories chimes with those of the young women who worked in the Merrimack Valley factories almost two centuries ago. *People have asked me, how can I tolerate this? Most of the people I work with come from up-country and use their pay to help the people back home. They're eighteen or nineteen, and they still have the energy to work the hours,* a young Thai woman says. *All we can think about is that we have to catch the bus. We have to work. We get home at 2 or 3 a.m. and wash our clothes and try to get some rest . . . My parents had twelve children. I was the youngest. Since I wasn't as good at school as my sister, and we couldn't all go, I let her be the one to go to school. I sacrificed since I wasn't as clever. I'd rather send money home . . . If we don't do the work, other people would . . . So it's like this, they lower prices—and still we sew . . . During the holidays we work all night, go home to shower, and come right back . . . If they catch you yawning they fine you 500 baht.* The factories can move away quickly, in the night, when the labor gets too expensive: *. . . then suddenly the factory closed down. I can't even understand why it closed. It can't be that there was no work. We were busy up until the very last day.*

Of everything contained in the original dream of Lawrence, Charles Storrow's dam has proved to be the most sturdy. It has required almost no repairs. The wooden fishways were occasionally replaced until a concrete one was built in 1917. In July 1915 a freshet carried away a portion of another dam on the Merrimack, and so they decided to secure the Lawrence dam crest with steel bars. In 1945 small cracks in several of the crest stones were repaired. During the 1936 flood, when the Merrimack rose over its bridges and washed tenements miles downstream, it overflowed the crest by nearly fourteen feet, and you could only distinguish the dam by a ripple in the flow of water. When the waters subsided it was as intact as ever. If I tell people, especially local people, that the Lawrence dam was once the largest in the Western world, they have trouble believing me.

In the world high above the roofs, the world of steeples and bell towers and smokestacks, it can seem as if the nineteenth century still exists. The hunkered power of Gothic and Romanesque revival churches had seemed such a natural match for the immigrant workers and the squat earth-tied cities, churches built partly of local brick and granite and oak, partly of marble from Italy and Yugoslavia, and deep-grained woods from Cuba and Brazil. But the drafty, cavernous interiors have proved impossible to heat, and even block and brick need upkeep. The parishes began to shrink after the work went to the Carolinas, and as children and grandchildren of the immigrants moved to the suburbs. I have no doubt that one day soon the local and the foreign, the fine-wrought and the rough-dressed, the tracery, woodwork, marbles, and granites with all their varying qualities, weights, and hefts, will lie for a moment smashed together in heaps of rubble before being packed into dumpsters and hauled away.

At street level, decay is evening out the old distinctions. There had been, when my mother was growing up, a marked difference between life on the hills of the city and that in the flats. The grand, ornate Victorians on the rises have been cut up into apartments now. Some are even abandoned; their windows are boarded up. They are slouching toward the tenements, and the tenement life is creeping up to meet them. New immigrants from the Dominican Republic, Puerto Rico, Cambodia are nesting in the old world. One high summer day as my mother and I were driving down Water Street the kids in the neighborhood had all spilled out into the street, their sandals flopping on the pavement as they ran beneath open windows full of music and chatter, past their parents fanning themselves on the stoops. My mother turned to me and said, "I don't know how people live here—the houses are so close together."

"But when you grew up here, your neighborhood was just as crowded."

"I know."

As for the granite quarries that helped to build the foundations of such cities, you can find vestiges of them if you follow the shore road along Cape Ann from Gloucester toward Rockport. You'll see all kinds of hammered stone along the way, in the curbing and foundations and walls and posts. You'll pass by many of the derelict granite pits, though you might not detect them with all the scrubby growth of seaside trees, and the houses tight together now. Eventually you'll arrive at Halibut Point State Park, site of the former Babson Farm Quarry, which has been filling with water for nearly a century, constantly, from underground springs and rain. If the water is a little salty, the salt is from sea spray and not from the sea itself. Mineral streaks stain the rock at the rim, plant life sprouts from the seams.

It's not that the rock ever ran out. The advent of asphalt, concrete, and steel—cheaper, faster, easier to transport—meant an end to the great demand for granite. Once the quarrying stopped, the pumps stopped. Water began to creep over the bottom ledges of the pits, then over the derelict ladders canted against them. Water rose over the quarrymen's exhaustion and ambition and anger at being exploited, over the 1879 strike for a ten-hour day and the 1899 strike for a nine-hour day. It rose also over their pride in the work: all the innovations that would never be taken further, the precision and technique that would never be handed down, and after a while, if the men looked back at where they'd once labored, they'd gaze into an absolute calm that reflected salt-stunted trees and a high, fair, twentieth-century sky. In their old age they led their horses to drink at the filled pits. They wet down their wagon wheels. In the palpable silence they could hear the surf again, and they let themselves believe that if the sea tosses up our losses, then the quarries keep them hidden. For decades after its closing in 1930 the Rockport Granite Company, the last owners of Babson Farm, had to keep the names of all their workers on file, and the dates each one worked, to determine the benefits due when silicosis—stonecutter's consumption—got the best of them. It almost always got the best of the later generation. Once the more efficient pneumatic drills replaced chisels, hammers, and quarrymen's spoons, dust flew everywhere, though mostly it hovered in front of them—its own silty gray twilight, level with their breath.

On Cape Ann, every once in a while, piles of chipped and discarded stone are hauled away to be used for drainage, or a quarry is reopened, the water pumped out, and a certain amount of granite for a particular job is cut from it, safely and efficiently, with state-of-the-art saws and drills. The workers flood water over the surfaces as they cut the stone to keep down the dust. They wear masks. One man works his own quarry still and cuts stone for the upscale home trade— the greens and sapstone pinks have a distinctive decorative grace—but the stone is rarely used for its strength, since there's steel for strength. Maybe only an old cutter can really feel the difference between the nostalgia for the surface and the certain massiveness of the block: *When they use stone now, it's different,* one of them says. *The stone is only one or one-and-a-quarter inches thick and they use it as facing. It's practically like hanging it in a frame. Our work was another way of doing something at another time.*

At Babson Farm men and women stroll along while schoolchildren play hide-and-seek or tag in a stunted oak woods littered with chunks of quarried stone. Metal clasps protrude from the rock, some of the edges are gouged with chisel marks. More than half the time in the quarries the granite split awry at a knot or along an unpredicted seam, and there were inaccurate cuts and slips in the hewing and hammering and dressing, so there is enough discarded stone at Halibut Point to form a mountainous pile—called a grout pile—which has been filled to create a heightened outlook. If you stand upon it on a low, cloudy day when the fog has socked in the coast, your eye narrows to what is beneath you, and all you can see is those hundreds of feet, it must be, of cast-off, half-squared stone, the discard of old use tumbled into a hard-edged beauty that now insists on itself like some socialist realist monument, with its sharpness and shadows and shades of gray. PLEASE DO NOT CLIMB ON THE SIDES OF THE GROUT PILE, a sign says. THE STONES ARE UNSTABLE AND VERY DANGEROUS. They look both sturdy and precarious, a force unfolding, and frozen, and forever falling down and down to the gray-green waters of the Gulf of Maine and the sea-washed stone along the tideline, to granite stained with salt life, with barnacles, fringed wrack and moss, which thrive on unpredictable surf and relentless tides—*the pounding of the surf is part of the normal life . . . the sea is not its enemy.* The stone smells of iron and brine, and the rise and run of the tides has worn it smooth as if to return it to its old molten state, to granite's first meaning: plutonic, after the god of the netherworld. *We are so easily baffled by appearances,* writes the poet Hugh MacDiarmid:

And do not realise that these stones are one with the stars.
It makes no difference to them whether they are high or low,
Mountain peak or ocean floor, palace or pigsty.
There are plenty of ruined buildings in the world but no
    ruined stones.

February, March, sometimes into April, after the snow melts back, I spend a couple of hours every afternoon pruning the apple trees on the slope in back of my house. It's my last real tie to the working life of the farm: three weeks' worth of work, five or six or seven trees a day—work apart from necessity now, since the orchard is just barely commercially viable: apples are produced more profitably in Washington State and China, and in most of New England the money is elsewhere. "One more bad year, and I'm selling," you hear the growers say. For now Dave takes care of the spraying and harvesting of the trees, but the wholesale price he can get for apples no longer warrants the expenses, and it won't be long before he, too, stops thinking of production. Even so, the orchard has stayed central to my idea of this place, and pruning is a little allegiance to what was, no more than that. You can tell by the way, in the last few years, I've gotten less businesslike about the work, taking my time as I look through the intricate branches into a milky blue spring sky. Every once in a while I let a branch or two at the top go—one that I know I ought to prune—just because I like the way it spirals away freely. Even so, as always, if I spend a long afternoon in the orchard I see a tangle in front of me when I close my eyes to sleep.

What the trees want is to send their many shoots upward as much as they can to gather all of the full sun. What I want—by lopping and sawing and weighing down limbs with water jugs if need be—is to keep the branches sturdy and horizontal, which encourages large fruit on every tier of the tree. So I make my way through the rows, sawing away the crowded centers, snipping off the water sprouts, puzzling out ideal shapes in my head, all the while talking to myself: "This one . . . that . . . not that one . . . how about—this . . . yes . . ." as I deliberate over competing branches, and lop whatever is growing toward the trunk or down or crossing another branch. After more than a quarter of a century the struggle has thickened into the shapes I see now: measured row after row of squat gray trunks and sturdy, spare branches with all the supple growth at the far edges insisting on its way in spite of the efforts of previous years—a beauty all its own. In the weeks after I've finished, however much it heartens me to see the buds gradually swelling and the forms of the trees softening, I always feel a little regret to think that soon the weird struggle—so apparent in their stripped-down life—will be hidden.

Last winter the first heavy snow fell before the ground froze, and snow kept falling—almost two feet in just one night—all through December, January, February. "An old-fashioned winter," everyone kept saying, as town after town ran down their snow removal coffers. We didn't see bare ground until March, and it was nearly April before I could get into the orchard to prune. Even then the snow in the shadows was over my knees: a winter hard on wildlife, and harder on the orchard. In my first walk through I saw that many of the lower branch tips had been bitten off by hungry deer—I'd seen them grazing the buds under the light of the full moons—and worse: starving mice had tunneled under the snow and gnawed away swaths of bark—six or eight inches—partially, or entirely, around the bases of some of the trees. They'd even nudged down through the soft ground and eaten bark beneath the soil line. I panicked when I saw it—the bark is the living part of the tree, and those that had been completely girdled would die. I quickly made my way through the rows to gain the extent of the damage: out of a little more than a hundred, numerous trees were partially damaged, and twenty, twenty-one, twenty-two were fully girdled.

Such a large sense of failure, though I knew there was little I could have done. With the winter ground unfrozen, not even the wire guards wrapped around some of the trees kept the mice from gnawing at the bark. The depth of that feeling of failure—and of responsibility that accompanied it—was a double sting because I'd started to believe I was freeing myself of the place and the past, but then and there I felt rooted to the ground every bit as much as I had immediately after my father's death years before. During his last days, when I was the daughter he'd wanted, taking care of the bills, tending to the house and farm needs, I remember also wishing—though never saying so—that he would in his last moments relent from the practical concerns of his life, let go of his control of everything. Maybe it was the part of me that is so much like him—the responsible one—that I dreamt of unmaking.

For all the conflicted feelings I had as I stood there, I was fairly sure the only thing to do was to let the trees stand and see which ones died off as the season progressed. My one hope was that they'd contain enough stored energy to put out a last crop of apples. My neighbor, who sometimes runs his dogs in the orchard, had larger hopes, though, and I happily believed him when he said it would be worth it to at least try to apply bridge grafts to the half dozen partially damaged trunks. He came by again a few days later—I remember just a little green was showing in the buds—to give it a try. Without his hounds running ahead of him with their bounding, scattered energy, he is a compact and deliberate man, patient, a hunter who brought the same intense concentration of the hunt to the task of grafting over the mice-bitten bark. He bent before each tree and surveyed the damage, peering in close through his wire-rimmed glasses, then backing away a bit and peering over the rims. He cut measures of slim new growth from branch tips, trimmed each end at a slant with a razor, and slipped one end under the bark at the upper edge of the wound and the other at the lower edge. Every three or so inches over each girdle he cobbled together these little conduits in hopes they'd reconnect the life of the roots to the tree above the wounds. He nailed them in place with brads, then daubed the grafts with tar to keep them from drying out.

I followed him as he worked, handing him a brad or the tub of tar when he needed it. Our talk was sporadic and casual: the trees, the winter, the deer, the birds, how the orchard would be giving way to time soon. "When I hunt up north," he said, "some of the most beautiful places I come across are the old orchards in the woods. The hillsides up there are full of them. There's always more light where they stand, and the soil is always a little richer, even after all the years. The wildlife love it." He was animated by the remembrance of it, and it lifted my spirits to hear him talk—it was something to imagine: all the human struggle let loose, with just a ghost of the old prunings to mark a place, while every year the Macs and Macouns and Northern Spies soften and drop and disintegrate to earth in a time beyond our own division of things into the beautiful, the vexing, the useful, when whatever we had cursed—scab and curculio—and whatever we had admired and cursed at the same time—such as deer—would thrive as they could. I thought of Thoreau's wild apples: *fruit of old trees that have been dying ever since I was a boy and are not yet dead, frequented only by the woodpecker and the squirrel . . .*

He loved the way apple trees were scattered through the countryside, remnants from a time when *vast straggling cider-*

orchards were planted, when men both ate and drank apples, when the pomace-heap was the only nursery, and trees cost nothing but the trouble of setting them out. Men could afford then to stick a tree by every wall-side and let it take its chance. Everything I know of orchards, and think beautiful— the measured rows of certain varieties trimmed without fail each year—Thoreau saw as marking the passing of what he loved. *Now that they have grafted trees, and pay a price for them,* he wrote, *they collect them into a plat by their houses, and fence them in,—and the end of it all will be that we shall be compelled to look for our apples in a barrel.* And after these orchards pass? Some of the newer ones in the region are planted in dwarf trees, kept no higher than five feet and set close together and strung on trellises like grapevines across the worn old hills. Even so, they are only a slight gesture. There's no real successor to the unreturning days.

Sometimes when it comes back, the wilderness that had been struggled against for so long really does seem assuaging. Maybe not at first, not when a hayfield goes uncut or the cattle aren't turned out to pasture, and the grass stalks stiffen and shatter. Then it can feel chastising, the way it's so easily released from its old order, as burrs and tickseed are carried in by sparrows, and fluff blows in on the wind. The following spring a scattering of primrose and vetch nose up among the clover and timothy, and as the months go on hawkweed and chicory force their way. Oxeye daisies, black-eyed Susans, butter-and-eggs—who knows anymore which are native and which came across the Atlantic in the ballast of ships? By late August, as the birds are flocking and the sun is beginning to wane, goldenrod surges and asters begin their late bloom while the umbels of the Queen Anne's lace wither and draw in. Milkweed pods open and their milkseed flies away. The old hayfield is now a tangle to walk through—like wading through an incoming tide—a confusion of clotted, leaning life where everything is both living and dying, and there is no order except the one imposed by the demand for striving. After a few years' time, when pine seedlings begin to cast shadows and the last of the hay dies back, the grass seeds become buried in an eternity of falling needles and leaves. Life crowds up high in the treetops, the lower branches of the pines grow brittle and bare in the scant light. Footfalls grow softer and more scarce within. Grown trees fall and molder to earth. Then it is almost forgiving in the way it lets you forget—even if it is not the great forest of the frontier, it asserts itself enough so that those without living memory are incredulous that there ever was a field.

My Aunt Bertha, when she had grown old, when the stone boundaries of her childhood had become labyrinths through the woods, walked among full-grown pines in the same place where, just decades before, cows had grazed. If it was December, in the afternoon—a brief and brilliant sun piercing its way through the trees—she would gather creeping partridgeberry and club moss to make a Christmas terrarium for the farmhouse kitchen. The stinging smell of bruised evergreen would come to life as she pulled up moss out of the cold duff. All over the forest floor they run, those mosses, a vestige of the immense forests of three hundred million years ago, forests that had once grown far taller than the pines we call *ours*. Massive stands of them had spored patiently and inefficiently, and when they couldn't compete with seed-bearing trees they evolved to persist close to the ground, shaded, nearly hidden. Over time the dead giants were buried where they'd fallen, and down millions of airless years they compressed into the coal beds we have brought to light. Now they're burning and drifting on the northwest wind, and falling in the rain.

A few weeks after my neighbor applied the bridge grafts to the apple trees, the blossoms on all of them—healthy and damaged alike—emerged pink, then whitened into full bloom. New leaves formed and hid the deer-bitten tips of the branches, and grass grew high enough to obscure both the grafts and the girdles, which had darkened with the weeks, anyway. Without the weird contortions of the branches to capture my attention, my eyes wandered to the air above the trees, to the flights of birds: goldfinches dipping in and out of the rows in wild undulations, the kingbird keeping itself aloft with rapid wingbeats as it searched the grass for food, the sparrow hawk hovering and crying, cardinals skirting the windbreak, the great swoops of tree swallows taking all the joy in flight, one undeterred heron passing over the orchard, and then over the woods. When a hawk drifted above the trees, the sparrows would flutter from the grass and hide in the branches, waiting silently. When the coyote trotted through, peremptory, they'd make a racket of warning.

Most were claiming territory and foraging for pine straw, old grass, twigs, and feathers to build their nests. Some of the smaller ones were vying for the half dozen birdhouses my neighbor had been putting around the perimeter of the orchard in the last several years. We always hoped for bluebirds, and we've had half a dozen pairs over time, though they are docile by nature, and everything that can will take the opportunity. Later in the season wrens fill the boxes with false nests full of sticks if nothing else has claimed them, or a pair of tree swallows skirls overhead, seeming to toss themselves on the wind to create a boundary around a box. They line their nest with feathers, and won't scare. If you lift the lid and peer in you'll see the female holding tight, tense: a bright eye deep in.

Even when bluebirds nest successfully sometimes their eggs are eaten by predators, or the chicks are attacked by house sparrows. I once saw a whole nest of nearly fledged chicks pecked to death—"by a crazy bachelor," my neighbor said. After such a failing you can see what defense makes of life: there's a large emptiness where the male bluebird once stood guarding the box—nothing, no kingbird teasing, no skirmishes with the swallows, just quiet. That absence is what you train your eye on for a time—though there are countless other nests still thriving, suspended tenuously from a branch, or saddled in a crook, or packed in a hollow bole—until one evening in a muggy dusk you hear the last sound of the day coming from the woods beyond: the fluting notes, clear and piercing, of a wood thrush—only one—calling from somewhere low in the pines. When I hear his singing I feel it coming straight toward me, and what with his solitariness, and me listening alone as the increasing dark extinguishes the boundary between the orchard and woods, it seems to suggest everything of *the inexpressible privacy of a life,—how silent and unambitious it is.*

There are some inheritances I know I'll never be able to shake. Some dream of order that won't stand for death in life. Dead-wood, which can look fine and defiant in the wild, ruins the idea when it's within bounds. Cultivation *is* a possession, an allegiance intertwined with necessity. In August, after the thrush grew silent, and I could smell the Astrachans on a light wind, the foliage on the girdled trees—even on the ones my neighbor had grafted—began to yellow. I couldn't imagine letting the dying remain through until spring, when they'd be skeletal amid healthy blossoming trees, so I marked them all with surveyor's tape before they lost their leaves entirely, and had them cut down. It took two men part of the morning to make a pile of brush to be chipped come March, and a smaller pile of wood to be cut into stove-length pieces. Strange: the trees that remained were still so insistent that, from a distance, I hardly noticed the skips in the rows where the damaged ones had been cut down.

Then came a winter that could not be more different from the one before. We were nearly snowless in January, and were already having rain in February. "I don't know, this is so weird," people said. I rarely saw the deer in the orchard, and the mice had their pick of other, easier food. Still, the light was spare as ever those late winter days, and by the time I settled down to work the sky was just beginning to lighten in the east. Quiet, the air above the orchard. The crowns of the trees, dense with last season's growth, seemed to be an impossible, wild tangle of work that lay ahead of me. A hawk sentried at the edge of the woods—a wary lookout all winter, finding the small life—was there when I looked up from my desk, and later when I walked out among the trees his high *keeeeeeer* claimed the ground, making me think to myself: *Not yours.*

Notes

Throughout *Clearing Land* I depended for agricultural information on Howard S. Russell's *A Long, Deep Furrow: Three Centuries of Farming in New England* (Hanover, N.H.: University Press of New England, 1982) and his *Indian New England Before the Mayflower* (Hanover, N.H.: University Press of New England, 1980) as well as William Cronon's *Changes in the Land: Indians, Colonists, and the Ecology of New England* (New York: Hill and Wang, 1983) and *Nature's Metropolis* (New York: Norton, 1991). *Larding the Lean Earth: Soil and Society in Nineteenth-Century America* (New York: Hill and Wang, 2002) by Steven Stoll and *New England Forests Through Time: Insights from the Harvard Forest Dioramas* (Cambridge, Mass.: Harvard University Press, 2000) by David R. Foster and John F. O'Keefe were also helpful. Jill Lepore's *The Name of War: King Philip's War and the Origins of American Identity* (New York: Vintage, 1999) was essential for my understanding of possession in both the colonial and Algonquin worlds. O. J. Reichman's *Konza Prairie: A Tallgrass Natural History* (Lawrence: University Press of Kansas, 1987) and Lauren Brown's books, *Grasses: An Identification Guide* (Boston: Houghton Mifflin, 1979) and *Grasslands: The Audubon Society Nature Guides* (New York: Alfred A. Knopf, 1985), illuminated the prairie and salt marsh habitats. Andro Linklater's *Measuring America: How an Untamed Wilderness Shaped the United States and Fulfilled the Promise of Democracy* (New York: Walker, 2002) helped me to understand the settlement of the prairie. John Fogg's *Recollections of a Salt Marsh Farmer*, edited by Eric Small (Seabrook, N.H.: Historical Society of Seabrook, 1983), made the salt hay harvest come alive.

I am grateful to Nathaniel Philbrick's *Away Offshore: Nantucket Island and Its People, 1602–1890* (Nantucket: Mill Hill Press, 1994) and Obed Macy's *History of Nantucket* (Boston: Hilliard, Gray, 1835) for historical information on Nantucket. Barbara Blau Chamblerlain's *These Fragile Outposts: A Geological Look at Cape Cod, Marthas Vineyard and Nantucket* (Yarmouth Port, Mass.: Parnassus Imprints, 1981) and *From Cape Cod to the Bay of Fundy: An Environmental Atlas of the Gulf of Maine* (Cambridge, Mass.: MIT Press, 1995), edited by Philip Conkling, were helpful for information on the geology of the island. The web site of the Nantucket Conservation Commission (www.nantucketconservation.com) provided me with information on the natural habitat of the Moors, as did *The Nature of Massachusetts* (Reading, Mass.: Addison-Wesley, 1996) by Christopher Leahy, John Hanson Mitchell, and Thomas Conuel. The Nantucket Historical Association was helpful with general research on the island.

Barbara H. Erkkila's *Hammers on Stone: A History of Cape Ann Granite* (Gloucester, Mass.: Peter Smith, 1987) helped with my understanding of nineteenth-century quarries. I'm also indebted to the Cape Ann Historical Association and the museum at Halibut Point State Park, Rockport, Massachusetts.

"Wilderness" owes much to *Into the Mountains* by Maggie Stier and Ron McAdow (Boston: Appalachian Mountain Club, 1995), *Logging Railroads of the White Mountains* by C. Francis Belcher (Boston: Appalachian Mountain Club, 1980), *Field Guide to the New England Alpine Summits* by Nancy G. Slack and Allison W. Bell (Boston: Appalachian Mountain Club, 1995), and *The Appalachian Mountain Club Guide to the White Mountains* (Boston: Appalachian Mountain Club, 1992). For the descriptions of the logging camps I relied on "A Logging Camp c. 1900" at the web site greatnorthwoods.org.

vii *Our signals from the past*: George Kubler, *The Shape of Time: Remarks on the History of Things* (New Haven: Yale University Press, 1962), 17–18.

1: INHERITANCE

3 *Horseman, pass by*: William Butler Yeats, "Under Ben Bulben," in *The Collected Poems of W. B. Yeats* (New York: Macmillan, 1956), 341–44.

4 *However it is*: Robert Frost, "In Hardwood Groves," in *The Collected Poems of Robert Frost* (New York: Holt, Rinehart, Winston, 1964), 37.

19 *Cultivators of the earth*: Thomas Jefferson in a 1785 letter from Paris to John Jay, in *Thomas Jefferson: Writings*, ed. Merrill D. Peterson (New York: Library of America, 1984), 818.

20 *That's what I despise*: John D. Fogg, *Recollections of a Salt Marsh Farmer*, ed. Eric Small (Seabrook, N.H.: Historical Society of Seabrook, 1983), 69.

2: AGRICULTURAL TIME

24 *They sounded the harbor*: William Bradford, *Of Plymouth Plantation, 1620–1647* (New York: Modern Library, 1981), 79–80.

24 *That neither he nor any of his should injure*: ibid., 88–89.

25 *how far these people were*: ibid., 92.

25 *of 100 and odd persons*: ibid., 85.

25 *stood them in great stead, showing them*: ibid., 94–95.

26 *The soil is for general*: William Wood, *New England's Prospect* (Amherst: University of Massachusetts Press, 1977), 33–35.

26 *We found after five or six years*: quoted in Howard S. Russell, *Indian New England Before the Mayflower* (Hanover, N.H.: University Press of New England, 1980), 119.

27 *The Indians are not able to make use*: quoted in Jill Lepore, *The Name of War: King Philip's War and the Origins of American Identity* (New York: Vintage, 1999), 76.

28 *The ploughmen ought to be men of intelligence*: quoted in Georges Duby, *Rural Economy and Country Life in the Medieval West*, trans. Cynthia Postan (Philadelphia: University of Pennsylvania Press, 1998), 387.

28 *a class of genuine full-time agriculturists*: Plato, *Timaeus and Critias*, trans. Desmond Lee (New York: Penguin, 1977), 134.

29 *the rich, soft soil*: ibid., 134.

29 *I have wondered*: René Dubos, "A Family of Landscapes," in *The Norton Anthology of Nature Writing*, ed. Robert Finch and John Elder (New York: Norton, 2002), 456.

30 *Every one of our commune*: quoted in Duby, 407–8.

30 *A man may travel many days*: quoted in Russell, 204.

31 *And to every person was given*: Bradford, 160–61.

32 *they began now highly to prize corn*: ibid., 160.

32 *For now as their stocks increased*: Bradford quoted in James Deetz and Patricia Scott Deetz, *The Times of Their Lives: Life, Love, and Death in the Plymouth Colony* (New York: Anchor Books, 2001), 79.

33 *There is so much hay ground in the country*: Wood, 34.

34 *Our beasts grow lousy*: quoted in John Stilgoe, *Common Landscape of America, 1580–1845* (New Haven: Yale University Press, 1982), 182.

34 *[They] took scythes out*: John Teal and Mildred Teal, *Life and Death of the Salt Marsh* (New York: Ballantine, 1969), 24–25.

35 *Rise free from care before dawn*: Henry David Thoreau, *Walden and Civil Disobedience* (New York: Penguin, 1983), 254–55.

36 *As for the Natiues*: Roger Williams quoted in Andro Linklater, *Measuring America: How an Untamed Wilderness Shaped the United States and Fulfilled the Promise of Democracy* (New York: Walker, 2002), 28.

36 *You have driven us out of our own Countrie*: quoted in Lepore, 95.

37 *Though English man hath provoked us to anger & wrath*: quoted in ibid., 69.

37 *You know, and we know*: quoted in ibid., 95.

38 *Colonial writers understood*: ibid., 74.

38 *In Narraganset, not one House*: quoted in ibid., 71.

39 *meat to the people*: quoted in ibid., 174.

39 *took off the Jaw*: quoted in ibid.

40 *The scene is truly savage*: quoted in Stilgoe, 173.

42 *He, who would wish to see America*: J. Hector St. John de Crèvecœur, *Letters from an American Farmer* (Oxford: Oxford University Press, 1997), 47, 51–52, 54.

42 *and thus the path is opened*: ibid., 54, 15, 27.

43 *I wish for a change*: ibid., 187, 196–99.

43 *Thus shall we metamorphose ourselves*: ibid., 211.

44 *Those who labour in the earth*: Jefferson, *Notes on the State of Virginia*, Query XIX, in *Writings*, 290.

44 *You are becoming farmers*: Jefferson, "To the Chiefs of the Cherokee Nation," in *Writings*, 561.

45 *I have been pleased to find*: Jefferson in a letter to Lafayette, April 11, 1787, in *Thomas Jefferson: The Farm and Garden Books*, ed. Robert C. Baron (Golden, Colo.: Fulcrum, 1987), 179.

46 *May 4. the blue ridge*: Jefferson, *The Farm and Garden Books*, 67.

48 *I think our governments will remain*: Jefferson in a letter to James Madison, December 20, 1787, in *Writings*, 918.

48 *There are but two means*: Jefferson quoted in Linklater, 213.

48 *Of prospect I have a rich profusion*: Jefferson in a letter to William Hamilton, July 1806, in *The Farm and Garden Books*, 191.

49 *The last 12 miles*: quoted in Lauren Brown, *Grasslands: The Audubon Society Nature Guides* (New York: Alfred A. Knopf, 1985), 38.

50 *The children of the American Revolution*: quoted in William Least Heat-Moon, *PrairyErth: A Deep Map* (Boston: Houghton Mifflin, 1991), 22.

50 *When I saw a settler's child*: quoted in Brown, 30.

50 *for you see no one*: Herman Melville, *Moby-Dick* (New York: Penguin, 1992), 379–80.

50 *a perch of poor soil*: Linklater, 16.

51 *Northward lys the lott*: quoted in ibid., 41.

51 *At the end of 22 yards*: ibid., 77.

52 *6 Chains, 60 links*: quoted in Joseph W. Ernst, *With Compass and Chain: Federal Land Surveyors in the Old Northwest, 1785–1816* (New York: Arno Press, 1979), 43.

52 *When you see how easy it is*: quoted in Linklater, 259.

53 *A uniform, invariable shape*: ibid., 174.

54 *peopled the Western States*: Jefferson quoted in Wendell Berry, *The Unsettling of America: Culture and Agriculture* (San Francisco: Sierra Club Books, 1997), 144.

55 *We must now place*: Jefferson, *Writings*, 1371.

57 *Emigrants too from the Mediterranean*: Jefferson, *The Farm and Garden Books*, 177.

63 *The unharming sharks*: Melville, 625.

3: THE NEW CITY

72 *I get along very well*: quoted in *Farm to Factory: Women's Letters, 1830–1860*, ed. Thomas Dublin (New York: Columbia University Press, 1993), 127.

73 *I arrived here safe and sound*: "Letters from Susan: letter first," in *The Lowell Offering: Writings by New England Mill Women (1840–45)*, ed. Benita Eisler (New York: Harper and Row, 1980), 46, 49.

73 *It is very hard indeed*: quoted in Dublin, 129.

74 *They contemn the calling*: quoted in ibid., 35.

74 *At the time of our voyage*: Henry David Thoreau, *A Week on the Concord and Merrimack Rivers* (Orleans, Mass.: Parnassus Imprints, 1987), 306–7.

77 *For two centuries the river*: J. W. Meader, *The Merrimack River: Its Source and Its Tributaries* (Boston: B. B. Russell, 1869), 289.

77 *In all the region*: Maurice B. Dorgan, *History of Lawrence, Massachusetts* (privately printed, 1924), 39, 41.

78 *The site had advantages*: Peter M. Molloy, *Nineteenth-Century Hy-*

dropower: Design and Construction of Lawrence Dam, 1845–1848, Winterthur Portfolio, vol. 15, no. 4, Winter 1980 (Henry Francis du Pont Winterthur Museum, 1980), 319.

79 *far and near:* J. S. Amherst and C. Adams, *Final Report on the Geology of Massachusetts* (Massachusetts Geological Survey, 1841), 270.

79 *no person shall dig:* Arthur W. Brayley, *History of the Granite Industry of New England* (Boston: National Assoc. of Granite Industries, 1913), 13.

80 *I see him there:* Robert Frost, "The Mending Wall," in *The Complete Poems,* 48.

80 *As it is from the surface:* Crèvecœur, p. 16.

82 *You can look through those:* quoted in Marion Knox, "The Glorious Day of Granite," in *Stone Slabs and Iron Men: The Deer Isle Granite Industry* (Stonington, Maine: Deer Isle Granite Museum, 1997), 12, 10.

83 *You have to take advantage:* quoted in ibid., 12.

83 *People couldn't imagine:* Barbara H. Erkkila, *Hammers on Stone: A History of Cape Ann Granite* (Gloucester, Mass.: Peter Smith, 1987), 3.

84 *My life and health:* quoted in Dublin, 126.

85 *It is not a home but a tool-box: The Report of the Lawrence Survey, 1911* (Andover, Mass.: White Fund, privately printed), 109.

85 *I used to hear my mother call:* quoted in Ardis Cameron, *Radicals of the Worst Sort: Laboring Women in Lawrence, Massachusetts, 1860–1912* (Urbana: University of Illinois Press, 1993), 91.

85 *You know how we workers:* quoted in ibid., 93.

4: ISLAND

89 *And I have sent them a shell:* Obed Macy, *History of Nantucket* (Boston: Hilliard, Gray, 1835), 263.

91 *Then it grew a crown:* Henry Moore and John Hedgecoe, *Henry Moore: My Ideas, Inspiration and Life as an Artist* (London: Collins & Brown, 1986), 157.

91 *The landscape is so bleak:* ibid., 156.

93 *The open talk that boomed Nantucket:* Florence Bennett Anderson, *A Grandfather for Benjamin Franklin* (Boston: Meador Publishing, 1940), 121.

94 *Liberty in America:* D. H. Lawrence, *Studies in Classic American Literature* (New York: Penguin Books, 1977), 13.

95 *The humanization of the Greek wilderness:* Dubos, 454–56.
96 *When first settled by the English:* Macy, 9–10.
96 *At the time of the settlement:* ibid., 10.
97 *The soil will not produce:* ibid., 112.
97 *a mere hillock:* Melville, 69.
97 *The island being owned:* Macy, 22.
98 *Who would have imagined:* Crèvecœur, 86.
99 *They found it so universally barren:* ibid., 92.
99 *When they come within our harbors:* quoted in Deetz and Deetz, 248.
99 *In the year 1690:* quoted in Macy, 33.
100 *these sea hermits:* Melville, 70–71.
101 *In that gale:* ibid., 116.
101 *and sometimes more than a dozen wrecks:* Henry David Thoreau, *Cape Cod* (Princeton: Princeton University Press, 1993), 125.
102 *Another . . . showed me, growing:* ibid., 90.
102 *something green growing:* ibid., 130.
102 *When I remarked to an old wrecker:* ibid., 126.
102 *The traveler stands:* J. H. Merryman, *The United States Lifesaving Service—1880* (Grand Junction, Colo.: Vista Books, 1989), 33.
105 *one could not:* Anton Chekhov, "Easter Eve," in *The Bishop and Other Stories,* trans. Constance Garnett (New York: Ecco Press, 1985), 49.
109 *I don't want pictures:* quoted in John Golding, *Paths to the Absolute: Mondrian, Malevich, Kandinsky, Pollock, Newman, Rothko, and Still* (Princeton: Princeton University Press, 2000), 46.
109 *[T]here has to be:* Adrienne Rich, "When We Dead Awaken: Writing as Re-Vision," in *On Lies, Secrets, and Silence: Selected Prose, 1966–1978* (New York: Norton, 1979), 43.
110 *I am here alone:* May Sarton, *Journal of a Solitude* (New York: Norton, 1992), 11.
112 *the left wing of the day:* Melville, 462.
113 *And sometimes, during northeast storms:* Fred Bosworth, *Last of the Curlews* (Washington, D.C.: Counterpoint Press, 1995), 54–55.
114 *We have built roads:* Peter Dunwiddie quoted in "Uncommon Ground" by Jill Evarts, *Cape Cod Life,* November 1998, 48.
116 *I was always aware that I was treading:* Rachel Carson, *The Edge of the Sea* (Boston: Mariner Books, 1998), 140.
117 *away off shore, more lonely:* Melville, 69.

5: GRANGE

120 *Have salt in yourselves*: Mark 9:50.

121 *They used to tell you*: John D. Fogg, *Recollections of a Salt Marsh Farmer*, ed. Eric Small (Seabrook, N.H.: Historical Society of Seabrook, 1983), 40.

122 *On the south side of the path*: ibid., 29.

122 *I would like to tell you*: ibid., 33.

123 *One afternoon he was going*: ibid., 65.

123 *They poled enough hay*: ibid., 33.

124 *That was the best part of the stacking*: ibid., 33.

126 *Attend to every duty promptly*: *Private Instructions to Officers and Members of the Patrons of Husbandry* (pamphlet, 1889), 20.

127 *To reach the Master's office*: ibid., 10.

132 *We live in a dream world*: George Monbiot, "With Eyes Wide Shut," *Manchester Guardian* (online), August 12, 2003.

135 *First it was a dirt road*: as quoted in Stilgoe, 87.

135 *Big farmers used their government checks*: Elizabeth Becker, "A New Villain in Free Trade: The Farmer on the Dole," *New York Times* (online), August 25, 2002.

135 *In Nebraska*: Timothy Egan, "Pastoral Poverty: The Seeds of Decline," *New York Times*, December 8, 2002, 3.

136 *In the complicated equation*: Monica Davey, "A Farmer Kills Another and Town Asks, How Did It Come to This?," *New York Times*, October 23, 2003, A20.

136 *We are a cross-section of the entire world*: Paul Auster, "The City and the Country," *New York Times* (online), September 11, 2002.

139 *We heard a distant tapping*: Edwin Muir, "The Horses," in *Selected Poems of Edwin Muir*, ed. T. S. Eliot (London: Faber and Faber, 1965), 86.

142 *sounding like the scream of a hawk*: Thoreau, *Walden*, 161–63.

143 *In 1836 there were in the garden*: Henry David Thoreau, "Wild Apples," in *The Natural History Essays* (Salt Lake City: Gibbs Smith, 1980), 204.

146 *The site of modern meat production*: Madeline Drexler, *Secret Agents: The Menace of Emerging Infections* (Washington, D.C.: Joseph Henry Press, 2002), 86.

6: WILDERNESS

148 *Those sublimer towers*: Melville, 209.

148 *Some part of the beholder*: Henry David Thoreau, *The Maine Woods* (Princeton: Princeton University Press, 1972), 64.

153 *This was that Earth*: ibid., 70–71.

156 *Though in many of its aspects*: Melville, 211.

158 *It is desperately clean work*: quoted in C. Francis Belcher, *Logging Railroads of the White Mountains* (Boston: Appalachian Mountain Club, 1980), 132.

159 *an area where the earth*: Wilderness Act, Public Law 88-577, Eighty-eighth Congress, S-4, September 3, 1964.

160 *In 1965 the trail was perfect*: quoted in "Challenges Taking Root on Appalachian Trail," *Boston Globe*, November 2, 1988, Metro section, B-3.

7: GHOST COUNTRIES

166 *The death of my father*: Thomas Merton, *The Seven Storey Mountain* (New York: Harcourt Brace Jovanovich, 1976), 85.

168 *People have asked me*: The quotations from women workers in Thailand are from the Bill Moyers *NOW* (PBS television series) program on globalization, September 5, 2003.

172 *When they use stone now*: Deer Isle, Maine, stoneworker Bob McGuffie as quoted in Knox, 13.

173 *the pounding of the surf*: Rachel Carson, *The Edge of the Sea* (Boston: Houghton Mifflin, Mariner Books, 1998), 55.

173 *We are so easily baffled*: Hugh MacDiarmid, "On a Raised Beach," in *Stony Limits and Scots Unbound and Other Poems* (Edinburgh: Castle Wynd Printers, 1956), 46.

177 *fruit of old trees*: Thoreau, "Wild Apples," 197.

177 *vast straggling*: ibid., 209.

178 *Now that they have grafted trees*: ibid.

181 *the inexpressible privacy*: Thoreau, "The Natural History of Massachusetts," in *The Natural History Essays*, 4.

Acknowledgments

I'm grateful to the MacDowell Colony for providing a place to work during the years it took to complete this book. Gratitude, also, to Blue Mountain Center and Wellspring House. Many thanks to my friends for their support, in particular to Sarah Blake for her insight, and to Elizabeth Brown for an early reading of "Squam" and her patient attention to detail. Thanks to Deanne Urmy, always, for her continued faith, to Cynthia Cannell for her unstinting efforts on behalf of my work, and to Becky Saletan at North Point Press, whose intuition and precision have guided these pages all along.